HAPPY THE SINGLE-HEARTED

Jesus' Spirit of Love and Chastity

by
Carol Cowgill

©Trinitas of Orange, 2009

The scripture quotations contained herein are from the Revised Standard Version Bible ©1971, 1977 by the Division of Christian Education of the National Council of churches of Christ in the USA. Used by permission. All rights reserved.

Contact:
Trinitas of Orange,
1111 Phoenix Canyon Rd.,
Arroyo Grande, CA 93420

DEDICATED TO ALL THE LOVERS OF GOD

Desirable and desired
longed for–
passion caught up and out–
you're also infinitely honored
precious, priceless
always in my arms and cherished,
says God.
Eros, bowing to Spirit
takes up the dance.

ESPECIALLY TO THOSE WHO SO GENEROUSLY READ AND CRITIQUED THE WORK IN PROGRESS

Christopher Dietz, OFM Conv.
Pedro V. Escobar, SJ
Elise Frederick
Fara Impastato, OP
Alicia Johnson

CONTENTS

FOREWORD i

I. THE SINGLE HEART

Introduction 2
1. Single Heart, Adulterous Heart 3
2. The Heart in God's Heart: the Beatitudes 11
3. The Covenanted Heart 22

II. SINGLENESS OF HEART: SUCCESSFULLY INTEGRATING BODY AND SPIRIT

Introduction 28
4. Beginnings: Capacity for Friendship, Marriage and Mission ...30
5. Beginnings: Voices: Augustine at Thirty 42
6. Beginnings: Dancing with Solomon 47
7. Mid-life: Becoming a Blessing for the World 58
8. Mid-life: Voices: Moira at Sixty 64
9. Mid-life: Dancing with Solomon 74
10. Full Maturity: Unmasked, Disarmed and Wholed 83
11 Full Maturity: Voices: Corazón at Ninety 87
12. Full Maturity: Dancing with Solomon–at Rest 101

III. THE MYSTERY AND METAPHORS OF SINGLE-HEARTEDNESS

Introduction		106
13.	I Have Called You Friends	109
14.	Sister and Brother to Me	116
15.	The Community of the Beloved	126
16.	Eunuchs for the Kingdom	135
17.	Bride of Christ	148
18.	Bridegroom of the Church	155
AFTERWORD		161
APPENDIX 1: Poetry		162
APPENDIX 2: My Own Story		165

FOREWORD

A person's attitudes or actions can be called Christian only when they flow from Christ's attitudes and actions. Chastity is about how body-spirit persons go about loving as Jesus does. Therefore any reflection on chastity must also be a reflection on all our relationships of love, just as any reflection on love must include the Christian single-heartedness of chastity. This book arose out of perception of the frustration of many young and mid-life adults seeking to grow spiritually. They are stymied by the silence that has descended on the issue of how someone who loves and is trying to follow Christ can actually become an integrated, loving person in a world that is seriously attempting to make sense of the complexity of a fully human sexuality, but is only partially successful because it does not yet know the mind and love of Jesus. Chastity is about successfully achieving body-spirit integration, says the *Catechism of the Catholic Church* (2337 ff). As we will see, chastity is one of the great misunderstood secrets of Christian spirituality, a spirituality founded on God's single-hearted love for us and his hope that we will return his love in kind and extend it to others. Trying to explain how this mystery of love is lived out by human beings does have its deep problems in an era in which so many people are sunk in self-preoccupation. How does one speak of chastity and single-hearted love to lost souls? How would one begin? This book, therefore, is directed to believing followers of Jesus, adults who have discovered God's love for them in Christ, who have taken on his inner attitudes, and who are looking for ways to make a more complete response of love. The intent of the book is, therefore, to surface some categories—some new, mostly old, all radical—within which to reflect on our experience of struggling toward an integrated love. The issues are raised in a variety of ways in the catechism, and the reader will find a great deal to reflect on in this section of that book and in its cross-references. Any future references to that work will be indicated by *CCC*.

This book cannot claim to be a master work on the subject; it is, hopefully, a seeding in the fertile soil of the lovers of God, to whom it is dedicated. The essays and poems in this book are, therefore, small motifs, suggestions, bridges for the reader's reflection. They flow from Christian experience but do not presume to exhaust it. In fact, the book needs to be completed by the reader's experience. This is the kind of book that is best prayed. To help this happen, a reflection guide is provided at the end of each chapter. These guides can be useful to both book groups and people who prefer to journal their experience. Space is provided for this in Appendix 2.

This said, we need to note first that it is clear in the gospels that Jesus' primary call is not to chastity as a moral discipline, but to single-hearted love. Christian chastity can be understood only within this call. Every Christian is called to single-heartedness, although the paths along which people are called are varied (married, single, temporarily single). This book explores some of the dimensions of this that have sunk into silence. The reader will notice that the author free-floats between references to single-heartedness, chastity and love. This is inevitable, as these are dimensions of a living love that infuses all dimension of a person's psyche. In living things, connective tissue is porous. In spiritual things, there is only one life flowing from God's Spirit, and its movement is not linear. Though it manifests itself variously, however, the love remains one. Moreover, the author has chosen to explore living love also along the paths of prayer, poetry and metaphor. This book will move by association and congruence, even when laying out apparent "laws" of spiritual development. For this reason some of the essays will also be interleaved with poetry and will refer back to each other. A reader who wants systematics or exclusively linear logic may want to skip the prayer-poetry chapters. Unless otherwise indicated, all poems are by Soledad Marinera. Poems adverted to but not quoted fully in the text will be found in Appendix 1.

Another note on vocabulary. Every culture has a clear vocabulary to express the things that it values. As there is no modern secular equivalent for what is meant by Christian chastity, we have to be aware that we will be reflecting together in a cultural vacuum. Historically, the committed single person who renounced marriage and sexual fulfillment altogether, the person dedicated to God in this extraordinarily exclusive way, was called a celibate. However, today the term "celibate" is used loosely to describe someone who is not currently in a sexual relationship, a sexually inactive person. So, for clarity's sake, in future we will speak interchangeably of "committed single," "celibate" or "consecrated celibate," when referring to those who remain unmarried for the Kingdom. The others will simply be called "single" or "unmarried." We will use the word "chastity," in the sense of integration of body and spirit, as in the *CCC*, above. Since this whole book attempts to raise the positive dimensions of Christian chastity, at least we Christians will be able to understand the mystery into which God is calling us.

A note on the structure of the book. Part I, *The Single Heart*, lays out some biblical dimensions of single-hearted love in order to base the discussion on a solid foundation. Part II, *Singleness of Heart: Successfully Integrating Body and Spirit*, touches on some of the developmental elements of the integration that chastity brings to love, and notes that success (chastity) lies at the end of the journey, not at its beginning, as we have often assumed. Each section of this model will consist of three chapters. First, an essay will raise the integration questions appropriate to the stage of development; this essay will be followed by a first-person account of how the integration was carried forward–an account reflecting the experience of early adulthood, mid-life and old age; the autobiographical essay will be followed by corresponding reflections on the Song of Solomon by Soledad Marinera, in which the believer-poet embarks on a journey toward single-heartedness. Part III, *The Mystery and Metaphors of Single-heartedness*, deals with six primary biblical metaphors by which we Christians try to express how chastity inserts us into the mystery of God's single-heartedness: friendship, brotherhood, community, eunuch-for-the-kingdom, bride of Christ, bridegroom of the Church. Further orientation to these concerns will be found in the introductions to each section.

A note on inclusive language. Every reasonable attempt has been made to avoid sexism. However, English-language pronouns force us to compromise. To avoid the formidably irritating he/shes, the paragraphs will simply alternate the gender. The reader can make necessary adjustments. The masculine pronoun will be used to refer to God so as to preserve the biblical perception of the Christian's participation in Christ's sonship. English has no grammatically neutral way of speaking of this mystery. Again, the reader is invited to make the adjustments corresponding to her or his theological perspective.

I

THE SINGLE HEART

INTRODUCTION

How did Jesus understand single-hearted love? He was steeped in the prophetic tradition, in which the heart was the symbol of the whole spiritual-religious enterprise. In this historical context, Yahweh was constantly complaining about the quality of his people's heart. As Jesus developed the tradition, he focused on the "single heart" of the human person who had all her religious priorities clear. The Beatitudes are this spiritual manifesto–and work toward the integration of righteousness, mercy and single-heartedness that shape his followers' attitude toward the world. And then he asked commitment, his radical challenge to his disciples to bind their hearts to God's, to commit themselves to him definitively (i.e., believe). These three elements–the centrality of the heart, having a God-heart turned to the world, and the heart's covenant with God are the springs from which Christian spirituality flows through a complex of watercourses until they are all gathered together in the great, deep river flowing through God's city. Then body and spirit will become one, a new heaven and a new earth.

1

Single Heart, Adulterous Heart

What we call spirituality, the Bible calls the heart. When we speak of the heart, we think of love as a complex of appreciation, desire, passion, compassion–a love full of affect, enthusiasm. To this, biblical writers concerned with the heart would add clarity of vision and purpose, choice of a path of life, and consistency in pursuing this path–all that we mean by mind and will. In the Bible, a heartless person would be a nitwit, a fool. In the biblical religious context, having a heart means a deliberate entering into covenant with Yahweh and the living out of this commitment by extending his merciful love to others. The history of Israel's heart in the Old Testament is pretty sad. It is hard, stubborn, blind, uncircumcised, even in the face of God's calling them to tenderheartedness, faithful-heartedness, intimate knowledge of himself. If there is a single note sung in God's name by the prophets, it is this: turn around, change your way of thinking, renew your covenant with me. Change your hearts, not your garments. Choose whom you will serve. So Old Testament spirituality is a spirituality of the heart in this broadest sense. The prayer that flows from this is *Create in me a clean heart, O God*–a single heart (Ps 51).

The prophets articulated a new thing in religion: that God would not be satisfied with any substitute for the loving heart–neither liturgical attendance, nor making of vows, nor conformist adoption of the religious mindset and mores of the society in which his people lived, nor mere compliance with religious law. Because the ambient religious practice was largely placation of divinized forces of nature, which regularly took obscene erotic forms, it was inevitable that participation in the cult of the local gods would be seen as religious adultery, unfaithfulness to the covenant that their hearts had made with Yahweh. Then by extension, all unfaithfulness of heart would be called adultery. Without understanding this, the reader of the Old Testament might conclude that the writers are obsessed with sex (fornication, adultery). Not at all. They are radically concerned with people's failure to take to heart that Yahweh alone was their lover and lord, as witnessed by their behavior, whether by worshiping other gods or by perpetrating rank injustices against the poor. Psalm 119 begins:

> *Happy are those whose way is blameless, who walk in the law of Yahweh.*
> *Happy are those who keep his decrees, who seek him with their whole heart,*
> *who also do no wrong, but walk in his ways.*

The rest of this very long psalm is a celebration of what it means to focus the heart happily. What we consider chastity, that often hard-won discipline of eros in the service of love, is dealt with only incidentally in the Old Testament, mostly in Proverbs 7, to warn the young to avoid the traps that eros can lay for them. The overarching concern of Proverbs is, however, the heart:

> *Trust in Yahweh with all your heart, and do not rely on your own insight.*
> *In all your ways acknowledge him, and he will make straight your paths* (3:5-6).

So the discipline of the heart needs to extend to all human loving. God's covenant love is to be the definitive pattern of human behavior; what God is calling us to in Scripture is the governing not only of erotic relationships, but also of friendship, family and even societal relationships. God-love, called *hesed* or *agape*, a total pouring out of self for the good of the other, is the definitive love. Our task is to make all other loves expressive of this.

So how did Christians get so fixated on sex? I suggest that our theological concerns are the result both of misreading biblical texts about the adulterous heart and of the fact that most of the commentators on scripture were young. Until the last century, life expectancy was about forty years, so that those who were writing were perhaps midway in the struggle to integrate their sexuality with other psychological and spiritual dimensions of the human soul. (Chastity is about this integration, as we have seen above). And since they were all young men, ways of self-control and redirection of sexual tension were major concerns. Most teachers, then, were the very youth to whom Proverbs was addressed. There seems to have been very little sense that true integration of body and spirit was achievable, so their concern somehow became non-adulterous behavior as a condition for leading a dignified, responsible and virtuous life in the world. But religious wisdom—a heart in covenant with God—got shorted in the discourse about chastity.

So we urgently need to start with the fresh view of the single heart. Jesus points the way in his observations about the adulterous heart in Matthew 5: 27-32:

> *You have heard that it was said, "You shall not commit adultery." But I say to you that everyone who looks at a woman with lust has already committed adultery with her in his heart. If your right eye causes you to sin, tear it out and throw it away; it is better for you to lose one of your members than for your whole body to be thrown into Gehenna. And if your right hand causes you to sin, cut it off and throw it away; it is better for you to lose one of your members than for your whole body to go into Gehenna. It was also said, "Whoever divorces his wife, let him give her a certificate of divorce." But I say to you that anyone who divorces*

> *his wife, except on the ground of unchastity, causes her to commit adultery; and whoever marries a divorced woman commits adultery.*

This is a passage that our generation often tries hard to deconstruct. If the heart is how we perceive reality and engage it, our generation is in deep trouble, for our public discourse is highly, almost exclusively eroticized. Our legacy from the nineteen-fifties and sixties, Kinsey and the sexual revolution, has redirected how we perceive chastity. Until then the societal norm was an idealized pragmatism: refrain from going all the way, fall in love, get married, orient sexuality responsibly toward parenting, preserve "family values" and maintain social order. With the new "science," the sixties shifted the question out of the area of moral convention or religious commitment, into an individualized search for pleasure. The moral norm became what "everyone" (defined, alas, by Kinsey and promoted by the media) does. So questions of purpose, intentionality, love and pursuit of the overarching good simply fell into oblivion. For the last fifty years to be sexy has been an end in itself. To attract the opposite sex is seen as the most important thing in life, and all one's energy is to be geared to this. Looking good has become looking young (fashions, cosmetics, even surgeries); the symbol of virility is the trophy (young) wife or priapic performance. Children are adopting this model at earlier and earlier ages, so that now even pre-schoolers are deliberately taught by the media how to act in sexually provocative ways.

What is really wrong with this–besides providing a very narrow focus on what it means to be a human being? The result of such waywardness of heart is that we have become a culture of erotic manipulation. We use the promise of genital sex as a self-aggrandizing inducement. At its worst, it allows the person to divinize himself: here I am, worship me for I am beautiful, sexually available, powerful, willing. There is nothing very subtle about all this, as we see in advertisements. I will pornographically flaunt or enhance my sex organs to trap you into caring about me, marrying me, providing for me, remaining infatuated with me, worshiping me. It is a way to keep the ego (even if reduced to the lowest form) front and center. The fact that this ego is probably very fragile is beside the point. The deeper unchastity is the idolatry that seeks to reduce others to its service. This is the core of the adulterous heart, an approach to reality that has dropped God out of the picture and substituted the self as the center. It is so imbedded in the social consciousness that it can be manipulated for commercial purposes. The auto industry that sells its products by draping the female form seductively over the body of the car. The romantic comedy that promotes casual sex in the name of friendship and works out the resultant problems in such a way that the whole approach is never called in question. Beauty contests. Makeovers. Weight-loss businesses. Fashion designers who try to transform women into beautiful boys—or worse, mannequins, seemingly sexless, but intentionally adulterous. What is the problem? The heart that says with L'Oréal: Be fascinated with me, "because I'm worth it." The heart that strives to be the object of "Obsession." Ironically but not surprisingly, we buy into the ultimate symbol of love, the heart-shaped diamond.

"So when the woman saw that the tree was good for food, and that it was a delight to the eyes, and that the tree was to be desired to make one wise, she took…gave some to her husband. Then the eyes of both were opened, and they knew that they were naked" (Gen 3: 6-7). The adulterous heart is foolish and naked. Foolish because it substitutes human wisdom for God's. Naked because, no matter how self-aggrandizing it is, without God it is weak and vulnerable. In this story Genesis presents the archetype of all human ills. The story is not about discovery of sexuality, as many think; it is about the loss of true sexuality in the loss of relationship with God, the loss of the heart. "You will be like God," the serpent had said. But humanity was deceived—thinking that likeness to God means substituting the autonomous self for the relationship to the loving creator. This, the author of Genesis proposes, is the real basis of Israel's faithlessness to Yahweh's covenant of love.

God's promise of new life, then, must take a new form:

> *A new heart I will give you, and a new spirit I will put within you; and I will remove from your body the heart of stone and give you a heart of flesh. I will put my spirit within you and make you follow my statutes and be careful to observe my ordinances. Then you shall live in the land that I gave to your ancestors; and you shall be my people and I will be your God (Ezek 26:36-38).*

This is the promise: adultery of the heart can be overcome and will be overcome by Christ. Jesus' gift of his Spirit to his friends means that the transformation to true worship of the Father is in the works. It also means that by our baptism (and in all its renewals) we have committed ourselves, returned whole-heartedly to God. So why do we not always act out of this commitment? Why do we still want to be worshiped?

Because our hearts are nitwits. Because our hearts are so unreflective that we scarcely know God personally. We have plenty of theological opinions, but almost no direct, intimate communication. This is what God complained of so bitterly: "For my people are foolish, they do not know me; they are stupid children, they have no understanding" (Jer 4: 22). If Gomer had known how unconditional Hosea's love was, would she have kept returning to prostitution? If Israel had truly known God in his personal commitment to them, would they have been so easily lured to the Baals? If Pharisees and priests in Jesus' day had known that God was looking for nothing but sheer merciful love, would they have remained so intransigent and self-aggrandizing?

What about ourselves? In our ignorance of God we, too, have made very important substitutions, as Henry Nouwen points out. *I am what I have* is the idolatrous cry of our greedy materialism. *I am what I can do* is the idolatrous cry of our attempts to use power over others for our own ends. *I am what people should desire* is the idolatrous cry of the unchaste. These concerns were the basis of Jesus' temptation in the desert. Note where his heart lay: true life is not found in bread; only the Father is to be worshiped; do not put God on trial. When society advertises a substitute for God, however, we easily get sucked in by the propaganda. And as our knowledge of God gets dimmer, our hearts shrivel.

"You have made us for yourself, O God, and our hearts are ever restless until they rest in you," St. Augustine said. And our hearts do not yet rest in God because we are ambivalent. We want to throw ourselves into God's love for us, as long as we can keep open the option that others will throw themselves at us. Covenant communion with God is not yet an absolute value in our lives. We offer him ourselves, then take the gift back in small change. In the whole sweep of our life or in tiny acts of bloody-mindedness, we are unfaithful to God's giving himself. Why? "Lest having him I must have naught besides," as a poet has it.

This is perhaps why Jesus says that looking lustfully is adultery itself. The heart that desires to use another person to aggrandize itself is out of synch with what it means to be a human within Jesus' relationship with the Father. We are called to God's kind of love. Any other way of relating to others is adulterous; by its self-absorption it adulterates God's love for his world. We need to challenge ourselves in this area. Truthfully–in all I did during the last month, what did I do primarily that people would desire me? Or desire me more than someone else? Since most of what we do lies deep within the movements of our heart, our adulterous hearts often do not want to see themselves truly. Nor God. Nor the dignity of another person. With the Laodiceans, we say "'I am rich, I have prospered, and I need nothing." While Jesus says, "You do not realize that you are wretched, pitiable, poor, blind and naked" (Rev 3: 17).

So what is the way out of this swamp? To be willing to set our ego aside and open ourselves to God's single-hearted love as it comes in Jesus. Then to impose on ourselves the discipline of refusing to act out of our adulterous impulses. This is the purification of heart that is the absolutely essential condition for growth. Once we lessen our unfaithfulness by not acting out of it, our hearts will become freer to see the possibilities that loving as God does opens up in us. Once God's love is awakened in us, singleness of heart is born and begins to grow. Its growth takes a lifetime.

REFLECTION GUIDE

What are the implications of committing yourself irrevocably to another person in a covenant of love? How are you living the commitment out? How is God living this commitment out with and in you?

In your opinion, what is the most destructive thing about adultery? Why does God use it as the metaphor for unbelief? How does this usage help you understand faith?

The opposite of single-heartedness is brutishness, failure to experience God humanly. What are the dehumanizing or depersonalizing qualities of the unchastity you see in yourself or around you?

In your experience of troubled relationships, how does wanting to play god in someone's life work itself out?

If you were God, satisfied with nothing less than single-hearted love from human beings, how would you go about helping people understand and correspond with your desire?

2

The Heart In God's Heart: The Beatitudes

Trying to understand God's revelation about the heart is always complicated by the challenge provided by the biblical translations we have to work with. For example, the ancient "clean of heart" became unintelligible and was retranslated as "pure of heart," giving rise to many treatises on chastity. Modern scripture scholars, in an attempt to refocus our attention, now sometimes translate it "single-hearted." What can be said about the nuances of each translation? In the Old Testament "clean" had ritual implications, something like the taboos of many societies, guaranteed by the gods and governing people's approach to them. The Old Testament is full of such requirements: abstention from certain foods, ceremonial washing, abstention from sex before serving in the temple or engaging in any God-directed activity, such as holy war, keeping away from corruption (diseased or dead flesh, especially). Since Jesus was clearly critical of fixation on what was clean or unclean, this term simply cannot convey his thought. "Pure," in its meaning of "uncontaminated," was better but continued the confusion, to the point that purity of heart and sexual abstinence became absolutely synonymous, again skewing Jesus' thought from the point he was trying to make. So "single-hearted" is the closest we have come to the meaning Jesus intended as he introduced the idea in the Beatitudes (see Matthew 5).

The Beatitudes are a poem. In Hebrew poetry the speaker was expected to be able to vary the images so as to make his point several times, intensifying it by repetition or contrast. As we see in the psalms, twice was the minimum, but a good poet could multiply the parallels three or four times. As we look at the Beatitudes, it is important to appreciate how many nuances Matthew perceives in Jesus' spiritual manifesto. Jesus' central concern is the joy of the kingdom. There is captivating richness of thought in all the nuances of this joy. "Blessed" carries nuances of happiness, good fortune, abundance. In the Old Testament, to bless Yahweh usually meant to thank him for all the good he has done for us (for example, Ps. 103). To be blessed was to find oneself the recipient of a great gift. The Beatitudes are the joyful songs of the grateful heart. Thus we could write them:

Lucky are the poor in spirit   *for theirs is the Kingdom of heaven*
Happy are those who mourn   *for they will be comforted*
Lucky are the meek   *for they will inherit the earth*
Happy are those who hunger and thirst for righteousness   *for they will be filled*
Lucky are the merciful   *for they will receive mercy*
Happy are the single-hearted   *for they will see God*
Lucky are the peace-makers   *for they will be called children of God*
Happy are those who are persecuted for righteousness' sake   *for theirs is the Kingdom of heaven*

First of all, we need to notice that Jesus' strongly reiterated, hence central, concern is the second half of each verse: God's Reign, the Kingdom of the Spirit, what God is actually doing in his world. So our primary focus needs to be on what is happening in each of us as God's attitudes enter our hearts through our awareness and our choices. With Jesus, we are trying to describe dimensions of communion with God. Secondly, we need to note that the "for" clauses are in what is called the divine-passive voice, by which we are to understand that the action is being performed by God. And the intent of the "will bes" is probably not a chronological future but an assurance of God's ongoing involvement. Thus we need to attend not only to the changes within us, but to the direct and ongoing action of God effecting these changes. Thus the reader can easily see how God reigns on earth–in comforting, in making humans responsible for creation, in giving fullness of life, in letting us experience God's merciful intervention in our life and our relationship with God as our Father. When God gets to do all this for us, his Kingdom comes–he is truly reigning in us.

So what is Jesus' point about the human situation in which God acts? In introducing his followers as the poor, he is tapping into the spirituality of the biblical *anawim*, those who are faithful to God but marginalized by society. In more contemporary terms, Jesus is deliberately counter-cultural. Our culture insists that we be self-sufficient, happy, aggressive, pragmatic, self-absorbed, unconcerned about spirit (harmony, communion with God), well-thought-of–and busy about deifying ourselves and our concerns, as we have already noted above. Jesus is proposing the life-giving alternatives to such dead ends.

What, then, is the inner consistency of all these elements of spirituality, the integration that throws light on our daily experience of the conflict between the spirituality of fallenness (the flesh) and the spirituality of Jesus and his friends? We need to become aware of how pervasive the problem actually is–as our interactions and entertainments make us aware of the split in insistent incarnations of human fallenness.

The poor

How do the media, especially TV, portray the poor, the homeless, the undocumented immigrants, social misfits, persons of a different color, religion, ethnicity, sexual orientation, the aged or persons with disabilities? If we look carefully, they are seldom personalized in our media. Mostly, they are proposed as a social problem to which we, as a society, respond with fear, avoidance, hatred, even when our responses are masked by a sense of fair play or good manners–or if we play it cool, with a nod and a wink. But who among the marginalized is seen as happy or truly blessed? Closer to home, how do we respond to our own experiences of being marginalized, in large or small situations where we clearly perceive that we do not matter? Often with shame, self-hatred or violence. Seldom with a single-hearted sense of privilege. Seldom with a sense that God is doing a great thing. And so often, with a sense of victimization, judging ourselves as others do, their "furtive whispers, niggling, nibbling calculations," as Soledad Marinera observes in *Cinderella* [Appendix 1].

Those who mourn

So no wonder we mourn. As the poor, we feel the injustice, the reduction of our dignity as children of God, not to mention as human beings. Mourning implies solidarity with all the marginalized, all those whom society deems unacceptable: those who drive clunkers, who don't own million-dollar houses, who do not look like models, who are not movers and shakers, who think they have no value, who cannot even get themselves together. To which we add our own misunderstanding of Jesus' way, usually in the form of discouragement with ourselves and our living of the good news. Not all mourning is good for us. The last, in fact, in an obstacle to single-heartedness, as it assumes that our response to the Spirit is something besides sheer gift. But such a deviation does highlight where happiness lies–in God's gift rather than in our high-level performance. We mourn because the values of our society lead us to doubt the value of the gift. In Psalm 73 the speaker, envying evildoers their easy life, regrets:

> *All in vain have I kept my heart clean and washed my hands in innocence…*
> *When my soul was embittered, when I was pricked in heart,*
> *I was stupid and ignorant, I was like a beast toward you.*

His working through this mourning finally takes the form of:

> *I am continually with you; and you hold my right hand.*
> *You guide me with your counsel, and afterward you will receive*
> *me to glory.*

It is all God's work. Those who mourn know, with the same psalmist, that it is good to be near God…to make the Lord Yahweh our refuge.

The meek

Clearly, then, Jesus wants us to understand something about how to respond to limitation. Not with shame or violence, as above. Nor with mistrust in our intrinsic self-worth, which our society calls into question in innumerable ways. Nor with self-hatred or hatred of those who are robbing us. Jesus calls for gentleness of response. The violent response (in its destructive, rather than its simply enthusiastic sense) is seldom from God. In the face of an intrinsic evil, lashing out makes sense. But we need to be sure that what is going on is truly evil. Jesus is saying that if, in our poverty and trust in God's Spirit, we have found our true worth, then we will change our perspective on what we consider so evil that we let it tear us away from union with God's desire that even the evildoer enjoy the fullness of life. Being willing and able to sort through these issues, having a discerning heart, will make us gentle. And, as we have already noted, the single heart is a discerning heart. Discerning, we can join St. Paul in knowing that nothing can separate us from the love of God (Rom 8: 31-39). Nothing. And if our union with God is absolute in Christ, then there is no absolute evil that can force us not to love. Our hearts are at rest.

Once we are at peace with God in our situations of limitation, we are able to move forward lovingly, to bring Christ's Spirit into the world in mercy, single-heartedness and peace-bringing.

Those who hunger and thirst for righteousness

The Beatitude linking our situation of limitation and our situation of power to change the world in Christ's Spirit, is hungering and thirsting for righteousness. "Righteousness" is a biblical term that indicates that a person is what she is meant to be. It implies peace, justice, innocence, good conduct and, in the New Testament, the freedom from sin that is the result of our being in Christ. In modern English, "righteousness" does not carry these meanings. "Sanctity" and "godliness" are not much closer. So today, perhaps, we need to use Paul's idea that, in Christ, we are children of God like Jesus and are guided by his Spirit. Lucky are the Spirit-led, says Jesus. We are what we are meant to be when our attitudes and actions are those of the Spirit of the Father and the Son, when we are Spirit-filled. Hungering for this means that it is a matter of life or death. Many of us Americans have never experienced any urgent hunger, but the often-invisible poor among us have—like the Guatemalan immigrant earning much too little to survive here, but insisting that life here is better because she gets to eat every day. Where are the moments that we are captivated by God with just such urgency? Every Christian has them—moments great and small when we long for a larger, deeper relationship with God, when we know that our souls will die without it. Unfortunately such moments are often lost, either because our hearts are not sensitive enough to become completely conscious of what is going on or because we cannot sustain such intensity. But in our better moments we know. We feel the battle between the habits of the adulterous heart and the Spirit's groaning to bring a new heart to birth. And we begin to respond. The temptation in this experience is to turn it off. Since our growth in spirituality is gradual and we are spoiled by living in a world of instantaneous everything, we are very impatient with hungers that go beyond our power to imagine or immediately satisfy: in this case it is the hunger of God himself, the longing of Father and Son to give and receive themselves infinitely. Created in this image, we can ultimately be satisfied with nothing less. This experience is the awakening that the spiritual masters say marks the shift from spiritual beginners to spiritual adults. Once perceived, it is a hunger that never leaves us, that keeps us moving further and further into Jesus and into the Trinity. It is a process that has no end in this life, because it is God's life itself. And it will underlie, impel, correct and transform us all in single-heartedness. Once this hunger and thirst are in motion we become capable of following the lead of God's Spirit in everything.

The merciful

We become capable, first of all, of following God's lead in showing mercy to everyone. From Old Testament times, mercy, *hesed*, refers to God's active will to save, a will that is always in play. Mercy goes beyond compassion by getting to work to change the situation that causes suffering—any kind of real need. It is mercy that rains down manna, that destroys enemies, that loves and comforts, that denounces evils. When God's loving is active in the world, things change. It is this mercy that St. Paul is referring to when he speaks of God's grace. We are saved by God's merciful intervention in Christ Jesus. We are grateful recipients of this mercy. This beatitude then invites us into the next phase. If God's mercy is joining us completely to Christ, then it is also joining us to Christ's mission to extend this mercy to everyone. To be doers of mercy and not just receivers. To be doers of love. Obviously this will not happen unless union with God is a matter of life or death for us, for, if we impose the obligation to help everyone on ourselves as some kind of moral imperative, we would soon be overwhelmed by the reality of our human limitations. But once we enter into God's thirsting for union with us and once Jesus guarantees the gift of his Spirit, then a merciful life becomes not only possible but normal. It guarantees that I will love effectually every person who enters my life. It may be a handful of people in my family, or all of Calcutta (as in the case of Mother Teresa), or the entire world, as Jesus does. The issue is not how many we help but how transparently we allow God to love them through us. The works of mercy are infinitely varied; because of human limitation, not all can be done by an individual (for example, the scholar is not likely to make a very good social worker, nor vice versa). The discerning heart sees what God wants to do in the moment; the merciful heart helps God out. And is grateful for the new relationship with God such collaboration opens up.

The single-hearted

If we are called to mercy, as Jesus' parable of the last judgment indicates (see Matthew 25), we can enter into the mercy of God's heart only by single-heartedness. To get to this point in Jesus' vision has taken us a while. Now that we know something of the physics of our universe and how each atom is a microcosm, we begin to appreciate single-heartedness. In every atom, the phenomena—electrons, gluons, strings, photons, quarks, and all the other particles that physicists keep puzzling over—are held together by a kind of dance of attraction and repulsion. An atom is the dynamic structuring of all these things. Singleness of heart, our experience of our relatedness to God in love, is the integrating force of our body-spirit. Singleness of heart is our entering into the Spirit's force field in our body-spirit. Once captivated by God, we can no longer be ourselves except in relation to him and his Spirit. Singleness of heart is how we go about viewing and responding to our world as Jesus does. Singleness of heart is like a GPS, an unerring homing in on the reality of what God and I are doing in the world. It cuts through and illumines the heart, laser-like. The single hearted, in their love for God, move beyond ambivalence. In a world in which people are torn apart by conflicting desires, conflicting demands and conflicting priorities, singleness of heart brings the freedom of being one. Unfortunately, instead of moving into love, many settle for easy answers, placebos to calm anxieties (ideologies and one-dimensional approaches to all problems, as we see on our talk shows and unfortunately sometimes in our pulpits—or in lives of unchastity). Singleness of heart does not avoid complexity and ambiguity; it organizes them around the mystery of God's loving and giving himself to his world as "the Lord of the here / and the there" (see Soledad Marinera, *Where* [Appendix 1]). Singleness of heart extends the gift outward and returns the gift in the form of the gift of self to God. It creates prophets and virgins, a reality to which we will return at greater length in Part III, below. The gift of single-heartedness is a gift of hope, the hope of true integration.

The peacemakers

The peaceableness of the meek as well as a single-hearted hungering and thirsting for righteousness must now take on the active form of bringing peace. In Scripture, peace lies in communion with God. Its existing in us means that, with Jesus, we are actively engaged in holding everyone within this communion. That our world is wildly, unpeaceably fragmented is apparent at every turn. But God's solution is to cure the fragmentation of the human heart by bringing each person into oneness with himself. This Beatitude is not so much about the issues that surround the Nobel Peace Prize, as about the challenge of treating each person–even if he is not focused on God–as God does, and of reconciling all who have strayed from integrity of heart and are frozen in opposition to love. Even self-proclaimed followers of Christ may not actually be led by Christ's Spirit. Knowing how to bring people into peace is a skill apparently in very short supply, for it demands that we simultaneously affirm and support the person in all his goodness and give him plenty of room to learn to love. It allows for complexity, for richness of gifts, as well as for the wisdom to respect the different rates at which people develop. The peacemakers bring the gift of unhurriedness into their world: they are the voice of God's loving affirmation: "You are precious in my eyes, and honored, and I love you" (Is 43: 4). We live in an unhappy world. People do not feel honored, cherished and protected, and so lash out in wars, in terrorism, and in attempts to exclude and demonize the weakest (the poor, those who mourn, the meek). Our task in Christ is to find ways to include them in God–to presume on this inclusion and act out of it. Peacemakers are not paranoid. Since we live in a country becoming rapidly more fearful and suspicious, we need to shift our point of view. When our way of seeing reality is God's, we will be able to help others along the paths of peace.

The persecuted

This Beatitude, too, becomes a hinge. The person who, because hungering and thirsting for God, is actively dispensing mercy, is refocusing all reality in God and is creating communion and community of the Spirit around herself—will be perceived as an oddball, a misfit. To the extent that the priorities of the prevailing culture are called into question, people will react. The human ego is weak. Today any point of view that diverges from one's own tends to be seen as hostile—and enmity results. With Jesus, the Christian may be perceived as dangerous, someone to be excluded by whatever means are at hand, often by mockery. This means that the Spirit-filled disciple will be marginalized, like the *anawim*, above. At another level, of course, but with the same sense of being graced, as Paul, who was grateful to be able to complete Jesus' suffering for his Body (Col 1: 24). It is the persecuted believer who is most in solidarity with the poor and who most concretely joins Jesus in his prophetic mission, who understands, through suffering it, that God is being opposed and that the Kingdom is perceived as a threat. Like the prophets, the persecuted Christian is the poor schnook caught in the middle—living the reality of God's life fully and feeling the refusal of this life as God does, as Jesus did—and with the same consequences. According to St. John, the final revelation—Jesus' "glory"—was that he loved to the end, even while he was not loved (Jn 13: 1, ff). God's kind of love, after all, does not demand a return in kind (although God would like such a return). It simply gives, because the fullness of life has to give itself. It offers, but, as with any offer, it leaves people free to turn it down. Then it waits. Lucky are those who wait in hope, knowing as Jesus did on the cross, that it was all in the Father's hands (Lk 23: 46). Peace is communion with God. The gift the persecuted give the world is the final word: nothing can separate us from the love of God. But on this solitary verge, love sweeps silent [see Soledad Marinera, *Love Silent Sweeping*, in Appendix 1].

It is with the wide lens of Jesus' spirituality in the Beatitudes that we can begin to focus our discussion of single-heartedness. What it looks like psychologically and spiritually, and how it develops will be the concerns of Part II.

REFLECTION GUIDE

Why do you think Jesus saw the joy of the Kingdom in situations that most consider evil or intolerable?

Describe for yourself the events that moved you to become a person hungering and thirsting to be Spirit-led.

Single-heartedness means that we are so captivated by Christ that we "can no longer be ourselves except in relation to him and his Spirit." What is the story of this bonding of yourself to him? What were the major stages of this process?

If we are made for single-heartedness, how do you account for the real ambivalence you experience? Where does the cure for this ambivalence lie?

Why is it inevitable that the Christian will find herself marginalized?

3

The Covenanted Heart

God is sheer steadfast love and he has revealed this love definitively in Jesus. The central Old Testament expression of God's love was the covenant. Its form is significant: it was a self-definition by way of relatedness: You are my people–I am your God. This is expressed in many ways, but perhaps most intimately by the names of the parties: Israel (Struggler-With-God) and Yahweh (I-Am-Here). As we see God revealing it, the covenant was not to be some theorizing of a historical given, but the engagement of two parties with names, persons who could be addressed directly at the center of who they were. The dramatic structure of the Old Testament lies in the tension between these names. Israel's most fundamental shift in faith lay in letting go of "God" perceived as some kind of force of nature to be fought to submission to Jacob's (and Israel's) self-interest, and discovering a divine Person who was entering into a relationship of love and expectation of a return of love:

> *Yahweh, Yahweh, a God merciful and gracious, slow to anger, and abounding in steadfast love and faithfulness, keeping steadfast love for thousands, forgiving iniquity and transgression and sin, but who will by no means clear the guilty"* (Ex 34: 6-7).

For 700 years, prophet after prophet called people to live their lives out of this relationship, with uneven response. Finally, the exile to

Babylon sparked a reconsideration of Yahweh's insistent call through the prophets and a return to "resting" in relationship with him.

The prophet Hosea was the most daring in articulating the qualities of this love in the concrete. Hosea's wife kept running away from him into prostitution and Hosea perceived that his situation paralleled that of Yahweh. The God who had chosen the people in love and committed himself to them forever was not appreciated or loved in kind. Through his marital woes, Hosea came to understand how far God's love went beyond human love. In fact, Yahweh's commitment went so far beyond that it transcended even God's own law that required killing an unfaithful wife. Instead, like God, Hosea kept going after her, trying to start over in a new exodus and new covenant. Says Yahweh: "I will allure her and bring her into the wilderness, and speak tenderly to her" (2: 14). In this, Hosea was challenging people to take a new look at what kind of person they had joined with: a God who loved them, wanted to share his life with them and would not leave them in their ignorance and ambivalence. A few verses further on, Yahweh renews the covenant with them. The imagery is that of marriage: "I will betroth you to me forever," he says. And then he goes on to list the bridal gifts he will bring to the commitment ceremony: righteousness, justice, steadfast love, mercy, faithfulness, intimate knowledge of him (2: 19-20). Because he lived it day in and day out with his wife and with his God, Hosea understood that our commitment to God could not remain mere cultural conformity. Covenant requires that our hearts assimilate all the qualities of God's heart. Given the chaos of our hearts, we would never be able to effect this assimilation by ourselves. Why not? Precisely because God's heart is greater than ours and we can scarcely even imagine what it would be like to love as he does. But the way into single-heartedness is there, clearly spelled out. To commit ourselves to God is to open ourselves to act out of God's kind of loving. When we are Spirit-led, as Jesus suggest in the beatitude of hungering and thirsting for justice, when we make a world in which God's love for all becomes palpable, when our commitment of love is absolute, when we extend ourselves to the needs of others, when we keep our hearts faithfully turned to God, then we will experience God with us. This is the covenant, and as Jesus teaches us, it is the Kingdom, God's Reign on earth.

It is our choice and our responsibility, for God has already made his choice. Like the Israelites, however, we do not always make the choice easily. Sometimes, secretly, we would like the Kingdom to lie outside us and come to earth like rain. But that we would choose to make it the center of all our decisions is a step we may not make readily. It is not just young people who fear such a commitment. The middle generation is too busy, too distracted by the materialities of life to pause to ask itself the life and death questions. We want the covenant, but would like it to be a one-way transaction: God will care for us and we will gratefully receive his blessings. But a return in kind?

Ezekiel, one of the prophets during the exile in Babylon, worrying about the ambivalence of the human heart, understood the hopefulness of God's heart. What you could not and cannot do, I can, says Yahweh: "A new heart I will give you, and new spirit I will put within you; and I will take out of your flesh the heart of stone and give you a heart of flesh" (36: 26). So five hundred years before the birth of Jesus, this promise gave rise to Judaism as we know it, a religion oriented to righteousness and holiness. Single-hearted love became the goal of every son of the Law.

By the time of Jesus the heart had again become fragmented. In the gospels, the focus of the Pharisees became not a heart expanding in love, but a safe keeping of the rules; not a covenant of love between God and people, but micromanaged behavior. It allowed a priest to walk past a wounded man in the road so as not to disqualify himself for service in the temple. It allowed a teacher to assert any anyone who did not abide by religious minutiae would not be heard by God. It allowed every man to thank God daily that he had not been born a soulless woman. The covenant had become the preserve of a spiritual elite. At the last supper Jesus proclaim that the new covenant is in effect "in my blood…poured out for many" (Mk 14: 24). Not for an elite but for everyone.

The new covenant has opened up to the new heart, that of Jesus himself. His commitment, as he stood in the river to be baptized by John, was to be the lamb of God on whom Yahweh has loaded everyone's iniquity (Is 53: 6). The covenant Jesus entered into with us at our baptism–to suffer all our chaos and lack of integration and free us to love–was the touchstone of all he did and taught. This solidarity reached its definitive expression in Jesus' giving us his life's blood to drink as the source and culmination of the covenant. In this transfusion, as we become one with Jesus' single-hearted love, we enter into his covenant with the Father. God's plan for the new heart is in effect. Righteousness, justice, steadfast love, mercy, faithfulness and intimate knowledge of God are now bound together in our love for Jesus. We live his righteousness, his justice, his steadfast love, his mercy, his faithfulness, and we enter into his experience of God as beloved Father. It is Jesus' wholeness that wholes our hearts; it is his Spirit that impels us to live out all the qualities of Jesus' loving concern for the world. The commitment implied in covenant no longer is merely a moral decision on our part: it is existential, who we really are; it is our name. With Jesus, we are God's beloved daughters and sons. In Jesus lies the final integration of body and spirit. The old heartless "I" no longer exists–only Christ in me and I in Christ (Gal 2:20). From this union, God's Kingdom itself, the life of Jesus, the perfume of Jesus' love flow over the earth, filling the house (Jn 12: 3). Mary of Bethany, lavishing perfumed oil on Jesus, thus becomes our model. The single-hearted lover gives a wide-open welcome, gives open-handedly and freely the most precious of God's gifts, because love must give itself or die.

At every Mass we gather to celebrate this mystery. We know that the final integration of body and spirit will happen, because it is happening. In our moments of conscious union with God in prayer, and in the love that flows from this union to the world around us. Jesus' love impels our choice. With Moses, he cries out to us: "Choose life!" (Dt 30: 19). Choosing life, then, demands that we struggle toward righteousness, justice, steadfast love, mercy, faithfulness, intimate knowledge of God, for not even God can make them ours if we do not move toward them. It demands that we discipline our hearts, reset our priorities toward God's kind of love. Jesus guarantees the rest.

REFLECTION GUIDE

The covenant is a committed relationship which every follower of Jesus has chosen to enter. What are the steps in your commitment to Jesus, from the beginning to today?

The gifts God is offering the single-hearted in Hosea are righteousness, justice, steadfast love, mercy, faithfulness and intimate knowledge of him. Which of these has been most characteristic of your spiritual journey?

What dynamic do you see operating in people who resist these gifts?

Is fear of commitment really the basic problem in committing to God in total love, or are other factors at work?

Who among your acquaintances best embodies this covenanted love? What are the signs of this love that most impact you?

II

SINGLENESS OF HEART: INTEGRATING BODY AND SPIRIT

INTRODUCTION

No one starts life single-hearted, since in every generation society effectually ensures that everyone assimilates the directions that it has taken, no matter how faulty. The parents of a thirty-year-old today were born in the 1950-1960s and were adolescents when the sexual revolution was in full swing–full swing, as in drifting like an unanchored boat. If they were Catholic, they may also have reaped the effects of religious training that called everything into question ideologically, a virtual religious training that, though theoretically calling for deep spiritual renewal, was often unmoored from an experiential relationship with God. The baby-boomers were a fractured generation–in a kind of spiritual big bang, exploding ever-outward, putting more and more psychic distance between the person and God, between one person and another. They were not the only generation to experience this. The fact is, no one starts life "hearted" in the biblical sense. We all begin as nitwits, totally vulnerable to any nonsense that promises us liberty, life and–more and more–ecstasy. Besides this, we are now sufficiently aware of psycho-sexual and psycho-social development to realize that everything that forms part of this development is part of a process of integration. We begin in pieces. Our life task is to become whole.

I propose that we need to look at the development into singleness of heart (chastity) at three stages: young adulthood (the twenty through thirties), mid-life (forty through sixties) and full maturity (old age), along with some introductory reflections on adolescence. What we will see is that, at each stage, single-heartedness involves different dimensions of the interaction of human beings with God and with one another, stages of the life of the spirit that centuries of spiritual writers have tried to guide us through. Having lost the worldview out of which they wrote, we find ourselves with a very difficult job to do: how to make sense of the journey we are taking with God in the twenty-first century and how to fit single-heartedness into the whole.

As a process of integration, or achieving singleness of heart, chastity becomes fully real only when the process of integration is successful. As in any human process, therefore, it develops in stages. Each stage will have its particular set of concerns, so chastity will reveal different faces as the Christian successfully negotiates the tasks of becoming an integrated human being. But first the warning. It is a mistake to apply any description of a living process too mechanically. Here we will be dealing with a simple model of psycho-sexual development. In former centuries spiritual masters dealt with stages of the interior life. When it comes to the Holy Spirit's work in us there is much overlap, regression, leaping ahead (with returns to gather up the pieces). Single-hearted love is the work God is doing in us. So as you read these chapters, read them critically. They are intended simply to be pointers, not straitjackets.

To get to the lived experience of the development of single-hearted love, stories and poems can be of help. The description of the tasks of each of three stages in this section of the book will be followed by a simple story of how integration actually happened, how three different persons struggled toward the integration of love. These autobiographical essays will be followed by corresponding prayer-poems in the collection *Soledad Dances with Solomon*, poems arising from Soledad Marinera's wrestling with single-heartedness as she reflects on the Song of Solomon. Love, after all, evokes a poetic response as well as a practical one. The numbers following the prayer-poems are the biblical chapter and verse being reflected on.

The reader can take from all this what illumines her own experience and use it to reflect on her own story. Space is provided in Appendix 2 for her to do this.

4

Beginnings
Capacity for Friendship,
Marriage and Mission

Adolescence and the capacity for friendship

The task of adolescence is to learn to love, to move out to others in friendship, to move out to Christ in friendship. Adolescents who are captivated by Christ and are taking their first steps into single-heartedness and trying to transform their way of living, really do exist. They face a quadruple challenge, however: the need to discover who they are, lack of models of Christian love, an over-eroticized culture, and hormonal turmoil. Hormone-driven, many try out the atheistic and debased models of love our society puts forth. They memorize lyrics of songs whose violence, promiscuity and misogyny cause even their baby-boom parents to cringe. Capable of idealism and free to choose their direction in life, they may suffer from lack of boundaries which their parents, in the name of freedom, did not set. They often isolate themselves in the media—music, anonymous (therefore prone to lying) e-chatting, games—as well as drugs and sex. Although, some recent studies indicate that Generation Y is staying closer to home and volunteering more, such behavior seems atypical. A more usual impression is of self-preoccupied experimentation with anything that remotely promises a rush. Then, with only their peers and the media as guides, they may make imprudent and self-destructive choices.

Not very different from any other generation of adolescents.

The really bad news in all of this is that our imaginings and our choices program our brains. In biblical terms, they change our hearts. Once neural pathways are formed and new pleasure receptors are created, our choices become habitual, setting off chemical reactions so as to condition us to aggressively seek out the pleasure associated with the activity. If the habit young people acquire is study and the pleasure they get is learning, then patterns of life-long learning are set up. A happy scenario. But if the intense pleasure centers associated with sex are activated, repeatedly stimulated and multiplied, addiction becomes likely. There are few learning addicts compared with the number of ecstasy addicts, whether this is found in drugs, exercise, or (mostly orgasmic) sex. Obsession and compulsion are the marks of the addicted, and these are the fruit of deciding that the value of what we want to do lies in the intensity of the pleasure it brings. As with any addiction, the fix needs to be stronger and stronger as the pleasure centers of the brain become more complex. And this happens not just as the effect of activity. New brain studies are showing that pleasure centers can also be activated by imagining and remembering sexual activity, what the Bible calls committing adultery in the heart. Spiritual masters have always known this, but since this generation is starting out rootless, it helps to have science back up the sages. The relationship between imagination and using others for pleasure seems to be the context out of which Jesus spoke of adultery in the heart, in Matthew 5, discussed in Chapter 1.

All cultures know that sexual license can derail one's life, and so have tried to inculcate rules about chastity. Everything from *Don't start; don't touch; don't dwell on it.* To *Learn to respect the other; learn to value the other person as a person and a friend; find plenty of common ground in addition to the purely sexual.* Thence to *Be responsible for your sexual behavior; refrain from sex when your partner is unwilling; refrain from sex if you could possibly transmit a disease; refrain from sex if your family planning or larger responsibilities could be compromised.*

The first set of concerns, the simply behavioral, can begin to be taught in childhood, though they are often neglected. Today, unfortunately, we seem to teach them only to protect children from sexual predators. But, as in simpler times, we try to keep children from acquiring habits of masturbation, too much sexual exploration or eroticized flirting. If they have not learned the consequences of their behavior in childhood, adolescents need to begin to understand them at this point in their development, or they will remain stunted.

Learning chastity, real integration of body and spirit, also means creative control of the imagination. We know adolescents are often obsessed with sex. Some of it is simply fascination with the forbidden unknown, sparked by puberty and the desire to be the center of the universe. The rest of it is the erotic conditioning that is coming in from family, friends and the various media. Young men and women differ in what stimulates them. The boys are grabbed by sights and smells that promise quick genital access and domination. This is why they are drawn to pornography, which is not only loveless, but very often takes forms of brutish violation of the woman. The girls are grabbed by the stories of loves that protect and cherish them, that create a future–the world of romances. To achieve this, they may infantilize themselves, reducing themselves to objects of male attention and desire. So the dance goes on, sometimes with roles reversed.

More specifically, however, the task of adolescent chastity and single-heartedness is learning how to respect and care about a person different from oneself. Sexual love, which can be a dimension of our relatedness to God, has to include appreciation of the other person as a person, seeing the other person as God does, as valuable, in herself, not just as an object of our desire. Acquiring a sex partner is not part of our call into the Christian communion of love. As we see today, there is still much confusion. Adolescents who are creating bonds of friendship and intimacy, as they need to do, have not yet developed either the sense of autonomy and responsibility or the self-control to integrate sexuality into their over-all relationship with God. So some elements of chastity keep hanging in limbo. College students talk about being friends-with-benefits: they like and perhaps even appreciate each other without seeking to marry, so pleasure each other in sexual ways. For them, sex has no future. This form of detour from chastity was generally referred to as fornication in the Bible. It was common enough then to require a series of commandments; it is common enough now to be the subject of innumerable comedies, soap operas and songs. Having liberated themselves from societal rules perceived as arbitrary, Americans see no problem with fornication. In this era of doublespeak we call it sexual fulfillment, and we are in denial about the sadness and sense of betrayal it brings with it.

Our adolescent Christians have so integrated this attitude that they, like their parents, expend enormous amounts of energy trying to twist the gospel into this mindset. As has every generation of adolescents, since history began. Every successful pleasuring strengthens the mindset, creates a habit of the heart. Every broken heart calls the whole process into question. Why do adolescents buy into all this? Because our society says that fornication is adult, mature, ideal. This is not new. Some fathers still think that adequate sex education is taking an adolescent son to a prostitute for initiation. No one seems upset by the cynical TV ad that presents a couple speaking:

> He: I have a sexually transmitted disease.
> She: And I don't.
> He: And we want to keep it that way by taking the advertised medicine [which the fine print and *sotto voce, prestissimo* commentary says will not cure the disease] and practicing "safe" sex.

But the habit of chastity can be learned. As a follower of Christ, think about what is good for the other person in God and refrain from seeking pleasure for its own sake. Self-giving love creates strategies for control and prevention. Easier said than done, as in the famous

Happy the Single-Hearted   33

Seinfeld episode of the friends' bet about who could refrain from masturbation the longest. When it was a question of changing habits, St. Ignatius Loyola had the people he directed keep a running tally of how often in a week they committed the sin in question. He was satisfied if the number of checks simply kept decreasing. Habits, after all, are learned coping skills, and, their hold on us lessens as we substitute other, more freeing, habits

So, on the behavioral level, how does one attain a Christian imagination? The advice to take a cold shower and put your mind on something else is not a permanent solution. Providing models of adult loving, making pastoral guidance available, helping the young person give himself for the good of another or for the good of society, are positive directions. But unless we give our young people the model of Jesus, we will shortchange them. How did Jesus–who, after all, also had to manage this integration–negotiate the complexity? In Jesus' day chastity was a value proposed and rigidly enforced by the society. Adolescence was brief, as marriages were arranged in the early teens. Although he chose not to marry, Jesus was attractive. He had many friends, men and women. He was a loving person. His body-spirit integration was successful–his love was single-hearted, as is clear everywhere in the gospels.

Adolescent body-spirit integration is developed in learning the value and skills of friendship. Openness with another, sharing important elements of one's life with another, helping one another out. Friendship in and of itself is not erotic, as eros implies centering only on what is pleasurable. Eros joined with friendship includes being in love, total surrender of oneself to the other in love, and establishing a family. No adolescent searching for herself is ready for this, as we know from our experiences of puppy love and the horrific consequences of sexual activity flowing from not valuing oneself as a person. The more completely the adolescent learns to live as a friend, non-erotically, with persons of both sexes, the more she will be able to grow into single-hearted love of everyone. The discovery of Jesus opens up the new possibility. At this stage, spiritually speaking, the adolescent is able to discover a relationship with Jesus and the Father that is friendly–shifting from a child's relationship with a parent into the easy, collaborative intimacy with a friend.

Precisely because friendship is a form of real love, engaging the person as a whole, it is easy for eros to enter in. Our hearts long for integration, after all, and the intricate network of our brains is always trying to bring everything together in one. If the adolescent is aware that the concerns of these two kinds of love need to be kept distinct from one another, he has a chance of growing up. However, if the adolescent is mindlessly sunk in eroticized everything, the trusty imagination will suggest eroticizing friendship. It is a temptation everyone has experienced–as the imagination sets off undesired physical responses that have nothing to do with the personal relationship one has forged. Then there come into play issues of not acting out of our impulses, the habit of restraint, of learning not to send out the signals of erotic availability (what used to be called modesty). This is why parents used to teach ways of dressing, speaking, joking, moving, touching that are sexually non-invitational, allowing the young person to act freely as a follower of Christ, respectful of others' dignity. Regardless of sexual orientation, the adolescent, urgently needs to learn this. It is the bulwark against promiscuity, the chaos that ensues when we get things all mixed up and we promise what we are not yet capable of giving, the gift of our self.

Young adulthood: choosing one's future and one's companions in this future

The twenties and thirties are the years of commitment. Psychologically the person has negotiated adolescence, knows who she is, and has learned the skills of intimacy and friendship, at least in a preliminary way. Religiously, friendship with Jesus is being firmly founded and progressively deepened. The habits of an aware and modest heart are in process of becoming stable. And the person knows in practice how to befriend others. The person is now ready to seek the companion of her life and marry.

However, from a spiritual point of view, there is much more at stake. The reason young adults are preoccupied with career and marriage is that they are laying a foundation for the whole of their adult life. The larger questions of who I am and who I want to become are now front and center. This is the time of the call into the future. For a Christian this means discerning what God is calling me to be in Christ. The believer lives in a perpetual state of recommitting himself to Christ, intentionally striving for single-heartedness. So, young adults ask themselves the deep questions: How does God want me to give myself in the world? What is the work God wants me to do? What are the gifts God has given me? What is he attracting me toward? The central question then becomes: In what kind of loving community can I better serve him in the world–in marriage or in singleness? This implies that a real spiritual awakening has begun–that oneness with God and with his plan for me in the world are truly matters of life and death–that I truly hunger and thirst for righteousness. The day that the young person can do this is the day he becomes an adult Christian.

In a perfect world, young people would be working for the Kingdom as articulated in the Beatitudes. They would be conscious and they would be critical of what society is telling them about happiness. They would be discerning for themselves. The Spiritual Exercises of St. Ignatius include a meditation on three kinds of people. This is a case study in which the individual discovers that what she has, has become an obstacle to her true following of Christ. The example used is money, but it can be any kind of good, material or spiritual. The first type of person simply never moves on the question. The second bargains with God, clinging to what she has, but trying to work out some arrangement with God that will put her conscience to rest, like tithing or using the money for the benefit of society. The third type is what Ignatius proposes: to pray for God to free her heart, act against the attachment to the good thing, and wait prayerfully for God to show her what to do about it. Though we do not always have such freedom, we are nonetheless called to be absolutely single-hearted, to be totally ready to move in whatever way God's Spirit breathes, especially in the choice of a permanent partner in life.

Young people often fear permanence. They have been raised in times of constant change and media distraction, by adults often multiply divorced, amid a breakdown of social responsibility for the weaker members of society. They cannot trust anyone absolutely, least of all themselves–their show of bravura notwithstanding. Studies indicate that when young people marry today, they expect the marriage to last seven years at best. The person who experiences Christ's choice of and commitment to him, however, is freed from this paralyzing hopelessness. He has experience of the ongoing liberation that is the work of Christ's Spirit in him. The Christian knows that he has a future in God and that God will open up a path to life. So, like the person in Ignatius' third example, he is willing to pray and wait until God shows him his path: celibacy for the Kingdom or marriage. He holds himself open to either. Once God makes his desire known, the young Christian can choose the path of serving the Reign of God within marriage and the family, or the path of service of God and his Kingdom on earth in a freely chosen singleness. In either case, God invites the young person. Believers can commit to either state without fear, for we know that the call and the strength to follow the call come straight from God. Jesus guarantees our fidelity, so we can enter into covenant. There are many metaphors of this choice of Christ, as we will see in Part III.

Persons called to marriage find that union with the beloved is drawing them deeper into God's kind of loving–of each other, of their children, of the people around them. They find God incarnate in family and friends; growing in love, in the thrill of discovery and being drawn into deeper appreciation of the spouse, even when sex gets boring or life gets exhausting. Persons called to consecrated singleness find that exclusive union with Christ the Beloved is drawing them deeper into God's kind of loving, an all-inclusive love for God and his dreams for the world. This is a searching for God directly–in God and with God moving into single-hearted love within the work God has given them.

Since not all people choose a spouse so explicitly in faith and many are single not by choice but only by circumstances, coming to awareness of the implications of their choices may take decades. Not all faith begins with clarity. Sometimes the Spirit works silently, impelling us in the direction God wills—and the full mystery opens up later. But the condition for full development is chastity: a freedom integrated in love of and commitment to the spouse—with God being the life partner of the committed single.

Such Spirit-led chastity of married people is an ideal, and it will be fire-tried by the realities of life. When fascination dies down, the ordinariness of the spouse comes to the fore, often giving rise to the seven-year itch. When the imagination reawakens and begins to search out other possibilities and an attractive person crosses one's path, a what-if is born, even a virtual what-if, as with the virtual flirting that takes place over the internet and that is never innocent or harmless. A grave problem is that impersonal sexual experience, fed by the culture, easily becomes obsessed with orgasm. The testing will also take place on the commitment front—when chastity takes the primary form of parenting, and physical and psychological intimacy may get lost: the sheer exhaustion of work and raising children cuts a person off from who she is in relation with her beloved. This is why wise marriage therapists and marriage encounters try to help couples back into conversation and rediscovery of each other's lovableness.

The consecrated celibate goes through much the same process. This is the time when the busyness of life easily obscures the intimacy of prayer, and the perception of one's loving relationship with God dims. Then the temptation to fill the void will come (for the consecrated celibate also lives in an eroticized world): judging oneself sterile because one has no children; loneliness because of lack of healthy friendships or communities; feeling alienated from one's body because sexual urges are not being gratified. It is a loss of the God-is-all, leading to an Is-this-all-there-is. And the ticking of the biological clock in both men and women often calls the freedom of the choice into question. Thus the shadow always looms: divorce, renunciation of vows—the sorry path of infidelity.

Integrity, faithfulness to one's commitment to the Beloved, becomes the commanding shape of chaste love as the person moves toward forty. And the pressing questions will continue. Who is this person whom I have invited into my soul? How am I experiencing Jesus present both in my call and my ongoing assent? As I try to model my values on God's, how am I shaping my life so as to be a blessing for the world? Also, what kind of person am I that I can say yes while experiencing my weakness and ineptitude? Am I beginning to take back the gift of myself to my spouse or to God the Beloved? If so, how? We are beginning to develop a more discerning heart. For this to happen, the questions specific to chastity must be raised early on. Am I letting God shape my approach to courtship, marriage or consecrated celibacy? Am I dating only persons who long for Christian marriage and have given a firm yes to God? If not, why not? Am I letting God choose the form my service of others will take, or am I maintaining firm control? Am I letting God open me to the wider needs of the world, or have I turned inward, to nesting in comfort? Am I letting God reveal to me how the life of contemplation has to be melded with a busy life? Have I found the shape of a spiritual support community? Am I allowing God to guide me as I parent my children into love?

For all, routine can easily set in. For me as a parent, children may become mind-numbing force fields of need; intimacy with spouse or community may require more energy than I want to expend. I begin to outgrow my friends, see myself constricted by my job, and ignored by the world. I love people and serve them, but get nothing back from them. "Who's feeding *me*?" becomes the cry. "Who loves *me*?" Though feeling overwhelmed, we know in moments of grace that we are God's and are searching for him along paths of distraction. In the night of transition to mid-life we may feel as if we are dying. Paradoxically, what is dying may well be our self-preoccupation: God is forcing us to think bigger. Especially when everyone we know is divorcing and the supports we counted on are no longer there.

For parents, as children get older and less dependent, there comes a resetting of priorities, such as allowing God to open up the wider vistas of the human task toward the social good or the universal good. For all, this is the time when the search for more (not to be reduced to a sexual itch) requires preparing oneself for the next phase. Once chastity has crossed the threshold into the freedom of a broader love, the person discovers the peace that brings wisdom, the clarity that Jesus refers to in the Beatitudes, singleness of heart. The Christian married person and the Christian committed celibate can begin to move freely into the depths of single-heartedness, where the Spirit breathes.

The task, then, of the twenties and thirties is to learn to love, as God does, those with whom we have chosen to spend our life. To spend ourselves in giving as well as in sharing. Our model for both paths is God, who is a loving community of mutual surrender, a God "in love," a Trinity in which each pours itself out for the other and who together overflow, creating a cosmos—everything good, as Genesis affirms.

REFLECTION GUIDE

As you negotiated the body-spirit integration during your adolescence and early adulthood, at what point did the process seem to break down? Why did this happen?

How did your commitment to God keep the process going?

By age 20 had you learned how to be a friend to others? Give examples of both successes and failures.

What was the future that opened for you during early adulthood and who were the companions you chose for this future?

What was the primary metaphor of your love for God (and others in God) during that period?

5

Beginnings
Voices
Augustine at Thirty

Thus I went on, sick and tormented, berating myself more bitterly than ever, turning and returning again into slavery, never cutting through, once and for all, the chain, worn down now but still resistant, that kept holding me back. All this time, Lord, you, in your rigorous mercy, kept pressing on in my deepest soul, flailing me with a combination of terror, shame and fear that if the final link of my chains were not broken, I would remain even more strongly tied down. I said to myself: "Yes, I will do it–right away." Saying this, I rushed to put it into action, but never actually did it. Yet at the same time I did not allow myself to return to my former sins. Feeling myself on the brink of liberation, I took a deep breath, then I tried again. I almost got there but did not get there; I almost grasped it but did not hold on to it. I could not make a definitive decision to die to this death and live toward life. The worst in me was more powerful–by sheer repetition–than the unfamiliar good. And the closer I came to becoming a new man, the greater my horror grew. This did not turn me back, it did not keep me from moving on, but it did keep me living suspended.

What held me back were the merest trifles, vanity of vanities, the memory of former girlfriends stirring up my animal passion by saying: "What are you leaving us for? From here on you can't ever take us with you. Never again will this or that action be allowed." And with this last phrase alone, what kind of behavior surfaced in my memory, Lord! Mercifully take away from me all these sordid seductions! These were already coming at me from some middle distance, not by way of direct confrontation, but from behind, trying to make me look back at them even as I fled them. But they only delayed my seizing on this new life and rushing in one fell swoop to where you were calling me. For fierce habit said to me: "Do you really think that you can live without all this?"

But their voice was becoming fainter and fainter. There ahead lay the destination I was moving toward yet trembled to reach: the chaste dignity of sexual Self-restraint, joyful, but calmly joyful. She affectionately invited me to approach without doubting, and reached out to embrace me with compassionate hands full of good role models. With Self-restraint there dwelt many: boys and girls, youths, people of every age and situation, worthy widows and women who conserved their virginity into white-haired old age. And I discovered that such Self-restraint was not sterile, but rather was a fruitful mother of the rejoicing children you gave her, Lord her Spouse. And she encouraged me with good-natured mocking: "Can't you do what all these have done? Because they could not have done it alone, but only the grace of their God and Lord. I am his gift, and they have received me from him. Why do you persist in relying on yourself, your unreliable self? Leap headlong, without hesitation, because you can't fall any lower. Fling yourself into him with total security; he will gather you to himself and heal you."

Thus spoke Self-restraint. Yet I was blushing deeply since I was still listening to the whispers of the vanities and I still hung suspended. And Self-restraint began again: "Deafen yourself to the filthy clamor of your base member so in need of disciplining, for the pleasures it offers are in opposition to God's law."

This debate churning ever in my heart was a pitched battle of myself against myself. And through all this, Alypius, always firmly at my side, was observing me silently and wondering how I would come through that crisis.

But when, by reflection, I hauled out from my most secret depths the whole mess of my wretchedness and perceived everything clearly, an immense storm broke in me that let loose a torrent of tears. So that I could give it free rein, with all its clamor and howls, I distanced myself from Alypius. Solitude is better for weeping, for no matter how I appreciated his presence, it was disturbing. I was already yours, and I did not know what I was feeling. I think that I felt the need to give vent in a voice already choked with tears, and so I got up. Astonished, Alypius remained where he was sitting, while I went to fling myself–I can't remember how–under a fig tree. I surrendered myself to tears, and from my eyes there flowed whole rivers as an acceptable sacrifice to you. I said a great deal along this line, if not in these precise words: *How long, O Lord? Will you remain angry with me forever? Forget our former iniquities!* (Ps 6: 3; 12: 2; 128: 2). For feeling myself still fettered to them, I was crying out in my wretchedness: When, when will I finally make a decision? Will I keep putting it off forever? Why not put an end right now to the brutishness of my life?

I was saying all this amid bitterly repentant tears. In the midst of all this, from next door I heard a child's voice (boy or girl, I don't know) repeatedly saying and chanting: "Pick up and read; pick up and read." At that point my mind quieted down and I began to ask myself very consciously whether I had ever heard children using such a chant in play. Controlling the force of my tears I then got up, sure that that voice had been God's command to me to open the book and read the first line my eyes settled on. Because I had recently heard that a gospel verse had guided Anthony, speaking directly to him: "Go, sell your possession, and give the money to the poor, and you will have treasure in heaven; then come, follow me" (Mt 19:21). Anthony followed this pronouncement and was converted to you.

Then I hurried back to where Alypius was still sitting, where I had left the book of the Apostle. I picked it up, opened it and silently read the section my eyes had lighted on. It said:

"Let us live honorably as in the day, not in reveling and drunkenness, not in debauchery and licentiousness, not in quarreling and jealousy. Instead, put on the Lord Jesus Christ, and make no provision for the flesh, to gratify its desires" (Rom 13: 13-14).

I had no desire to read further. For as I finished reading the last sentence, an absolutely certain light filled my heart, scattering at one fell swoop the darkness of my doubts. So I closed the book, marking the passage with my finger or some other way, I don't remember how. Now at peace, I told Alypius everything that had happened. He shared with me what he was experiencing spiritually, experiences I was unaware of. He wanted to see what I had read. Reviewing it, he went beyond the place I had paused. What followed was: "Welcome those who are weak in faith" (Rom 14:1). He applied these words to himself and told me why: that it was good and congruent with the thrust of his spiritual life, which long before had outstripped mine and left me behind. Without fuss or delay he joined me. We next went to see my mother and told her about our decision, and she was happy. But when we told her all the details of the story, her exultation was triumphant. She began to praise you who are powerful enough to give us more that we can ask and understand (Eph 3:29). For she saw surely that that you had given me much more than what she, with groans and tears, used to ask you for. This is how you converted me to you, so that I gave up chasing women and I left behind everything this world hopes for. In this way, I stood up to that measure of faith that you had revealed to her for so many years. Her mourning was turned into rejoicing, into a rejoicing much greater than she had desired and much more chaste and lovable than she could have expected from any grandchildren I might have given her.

St. Augustine, *Confessions*, VIII. 11-12

REFLECTION GUIDE

As you read of Augustine's struggle, identify the primary issues of chastity he was dealing with?

What were Augustine's primary motives in his struggle to change?

Does knowing that Augustine had a very deep gift for friendship give you any insight into the particularities of the struggle? Explain.

If you had been Augustine's spiritual director, how would you have guided him through the turmoil of his conversion toward single-heartedness?

6

Beginnings
Dancing with Solomon

LET HIM KISS ME

Soledad:

Where's the kiss by which you promise to waken me
to Spirit's fire blazing face to face
as you bind yourself to me in covenant
(while I–doubtful, unsure of love–
semi-assent to a semi-remembered promise)
and carry me across the threshold
to my soul's center,
where I'm to learn loving
by joining you in your kiss of the Father?
I wait for what's beyond
(me? hope? all probability?),
dreading the promise you make
To one unready for love of you,
the ever-stranger Stranger
and Lover of my soul.
Can your kiss create surrender?

Soledad and Jesus:

In the presence of the perfume of your name
spreading through me,
holding my microcosmic heart spellbound
by most primitive and spirited sense–
you perfume everything you touch in love,
transforming the malodorous, unwashed,
bathing my soul in nuance of our Spirit,
the banquet
of your kissing me
tasted.

Draw me deeper into that kiss, Abba,
where you and I abide
in singing surrender.
Make me your kiss
to each of these thirsting for the wine of your mouth
and covenant of love pouring free from mine,
subtly spiced by our consenting Spirit.

The Father:

Turn toward each other, not toward me,
for the surge of desire between you,
hanging on that kiss,
is my face and the force-field of our threefold love:
surrender unneeded in the outrush of our longing.
1:2

HAD I TENDED ONLY MY OWN

Why are you calling me to you?
I'm not like others who love you cleanly
without contorting their soul into celtic knots–
no simplicity, integrity or grace here–
as every hostile hypercritic eye can clearly see.
I've only the weariness of my heart's darkness,
which your voice can burn away–
wordless–
and which, when you disappear,
flashes into an ice storm,
leaving me exhausted,
homesick,
hopeless
that you're the love of my loveless heart.
Calling me nowhere.
1:6

AS A LOTUS MY LOVE

Darkness
stills the hostile, hypercritic eye
dilated far beyond the power to see
the beauty that I'm making in you,
the splendor of my Spirit's shaping you.
Stop looking, for your eyes,
too open to the light,
are blinded. Close them
and let your heart
gently
open its petals
to the dew and the sun
in the perfume of my peaceful presence
embodied in you,
pouring through every pore.
2:2

I AM WEAK WITH LOVEMAKING

If I surrendered to your love for me
I'd go crazy in this desert,
for the loss would be intolerable.
And loss there would be,
addiction guaranteeing it:
nowhere to go for a fix,
nothing even close,
no one who loves my soul.
No, then.
Don't even give me a taste.
I've no strength to sustain
any intercourse with you
in this barren faith.
Don't start,
for I can't make it to the finish
or even the qualifying rounds.
2:5

DO NOT FORCE LOVE, 1

No matter what you do, I'll never go away,
for I can wait
till your awakening moves beyond
the sorry remnants of your fear of pain
into a transparency like mine.
Then together
we'll rush
into the Father's laughter.
We're all waiting, so hurry, Soledad:
urgent our need of you.
2:7

IN CREVICES

When I let them strip me of my soul,
all those who could not love me,
in my shame
I concealed myself high in the mountains'
perpetual winter–
a lifetime's work–
isolated
unloved.
Now, as your love calls me out
and calls me lovable,
I cannot rise,
too fearful that this tiny hope,
too,
will be stripped naked
and flash-frozen.
2:14

LISTEN

You of the word
you're speaking
from the secret place of Spirit's spring
soaking into the desert's emptiness
and calling me at least to look around
at flowers everywhere bursting alive
into shimmering splendor.
All I see
with wintry eyes
is the deafening danger of frost-blight.
2:12

YOUR VOICE IS DELIGHTFUL

If you'll settle for the voice I have,
Shattered by all the rocks it has to echo from,
I'll set the terms:
that first you name me the demons
poaching and squatting at my every turn,
or, another way,
that first I feel my wintriness melt
by some urgent willingness of love
just enough to soften this doubt
that it's you who are calling,
speaking to me
only
of what you've done
in naming me Beauty and Love.
2:14

ON THE CLEFT MOUNTAIN

We are each other's.
You see the quickening power of your love,
while I want to stay on the rocky heights
where only you can come.
And though you'll call me there,
you're not at home—
nor I, if not in you.
So must I choose to leave,
to find you in the flower fields
of folk transfigured by your love?
And then, fearless,
conditions laid to rest,
we'll be oned in a million?
2:14

DO NOT FORCE LOVE, 2

Manipulation's out.
The weary hesitation of your timid heart
has to swallow its despair
before it ventures out
from the safe silence
of solitary confinement,
untouchable.
I wait, unrecognized,
till love lays your blinding soul-cramp,
Soledad,
at your soul's hearth.
3:5

COME FROM LEBANON

Astringency of pine and sage and cedar's
like a great freshwater current in the sea.
How can I be tamed to sweetness?
4:8

LIKE A COLUMN OF SMOKE

A promised honeymoon in a dusty plain,
this column of smoke
(and what by night?)–
back at the beginning,
before I got lost in my arrogance and unheeding
and before you let the consequences roll over me,
driving me to the silence of the mountain
of solitude,
your home.
What's this display of power
and proclamation of my beauty?
I will never be the untouched darling of your song.
I bring not only the dryness
of too many days and nights of homelessness,
but a change of taste,
for the lushness of your song
cannot move this mountain-dwelling heart.
Be Bach to me, not Brahms.
If the day of beauty come, I'll join the song.
Till then, leave me where I have to be.
3:6

I HAVE ENTERED MY GARDEN

I'm not asking you to come into the garden,
but to be for me paradisal:
my Spirit flowing fresh within you
is recreating the world in you,
is bringing my yes to the Father to birth in you,
is doing what you do not so much as suspect in you,
there, among the giant, storm-sustaining cedars
that are your proper home.
Come to me and bring Lebanon—my Spirit—with you.
Why ever would I wish you other?
4:16

NORTH WIND, BREATHE

Stop lying, Soledad.
You have had glimpses of your greatness,
of what my love is doing there in you
where you cannot always see—
that spacious place of silence in you
where the winds blow free
and where you want to be,
there, in Lebanon.
4:16

JERUSALEM GIRLS, COME OUT

The city's not the place.
We all must go, in you,
to where the Spirit breathes
and cascades through the gorge,
leaving us suspended and aware.
Only there
can you be king,
and all of us alive.
5:8

REFLECTION GUIDE

In Let Him Kiss Me *Soledad Marinera raises the meaning of the Trinitarian love of God in the metaphor of the kiss. How did you experience this surrender in your youth?*

What is the beauty that God sees in you?

In In Crevices *and* Do Not Force Love, 2, *the author deals with the failure to integrate love for herself. Why is it important to pinpoint this problem—and what is the obstacle to integration reflected in these poems? How does integration occur?*

According to the last three poems, what is the greatness God has been creating in us?

7

Mid-Life
Becoming a Blessing for the World

At mid-life, if the person has successfully negotiated the paths of intimacy, friendship and surrender in love, the fragments of desires and choices begin to come together. Single-hearted desire to love God in everything is leading to being able to recognize him in everything and everyone. Part of this vision is learning that God is at work in all the relationships of love in our lives and seeing how the interaction of God and self has been life-giving for all those we love and care for. But, as with learning to love, this will also be a process. Now Christian chastity will take the form of new, broader and more mature possibilities. The paths we followed in our twenties and thirties will now need to be reevaluated in the light of changed circumstances: fledging the kids; enough financial stability to consider kinds of work which God has been preparing us for, but which pay less–or not at all; radical change of direction towards ministry or contemplative life. This is also the time when the integration of masculine and feminine dimensions of the personality ordinarily takes place. This is when the married person can enter into the life style of the consecrated celibate. What is the Kingdom today? Along what new path is God calling me (us)? How can I (or we) prepare myself for new ways of giving life. Psychologists talk about mentoring, passing skills on and ultimately handing over the task to the next generation.

There will be tensions–the mid-life crisis. Questions rise. Once I have learned to give myself truly to the other (God, friend, spouse, children, community) and no longer define myself by the qualities or achievements that make me desirable, what will become of my idea of myself? At mid-life, truly integrated chastity is a progressive moving of my ego from the center of my concern, a change from perceiving myself in terms of my desirability or my ability to produce. At mid-life I redefine myself in faith: with Jesus, I am God's beloved daughter or son. Since this is the source of my worth, attracting others into my orbit so as to affirm my worth makes less and less sense. Single-heartedness takes the shape of John the Baptist's conviction: "He must increase, but I must decrease" (Jn 3: 30).

The transition, however, can be difficult, as we see in the obsession that leads mid-lifers to cling to the appearance of youth: searching for remedies for wrinkles, balding, grey hair, flab, erectile dysfunction–endless fear of a diminished life. But why should all this be feared by Christians? Such fear is often the result of not letting God affirm our worth as a person. We are still equating sexuality with with desirability and autonomous potency, in both masculine and feminine forms: I can impose my life on the world or I can force you to desire/love me. And since we sometimes do not search deeper into Jesus' vision of reality and his affirmation of us as his beloved (flabby, bald, grey, impotent though we be), we may well feel that we have come to the end, death. The medieval depictions of a woman before a mirror that reflected only a skull, a caution against vanity, now becomes a lived experience–for men as well as for women. And it is a dark night, the death of a half century of living only half a life. The solution for the anxiety of the transition is a deeper oneness with Jesus and entering more deeply into his way of thinking and acting. The task of mid-life is not so much the choice of a path but much more a reexamining of our attitudes by the single light of the love into which God is calling us. For very active people, contemplation needs to open up: praying the scriptures, discerning the action of

Jesus' Spirit in the every day. For very contemplative people, service will be the road to integration. Men will need to allow their feminine sides to emerge, as women, their masculine sides. In personalities, the neglected side of the introvert/extrovert, sensory/intuitive, thinking/feeling, judging/perceptive dyads will be encouraged to emerge, so as to balance our approach to the world. When engaged in faith, this is a time of great spiritual growth, integration and even transformation. It is the time of bearing the Spirit's fruit.

In all this our single-heartedness will be tried. For example, single-heartedness leads us to let go of trying to control people, especially our adult children, and leads us to follow God's lead in helping others develop, willingly sharing skills and jobs with others in mentoring. It opens our hearts to the needs of a world unbelievably larger than our world of making a living and raising a family. It creates the open-heartedness that allows God to lead us in totally new directions.

But growth may also require forms of painful pruning–or with, Peter caught in the storm, being dragged under by life that seems sometimes to be, as Soledad Marinera puts it in *Here I Am*, nothing less than the "screaming vortices of hell." The abyss includes the last grasping at things as a security, as talismans against mortality (the sports car; the trendy whatevers that advertisers try to sell us; the wasting of our time and resources on looking good to others; the trading in of the life of service for a life of getting our own way). And we know the signs: preoccupation with our appearance; addiction to chat rooms or even pornography; estrangement from or unavailability (in its many forms) to the family; neglect of prayer. When the soul is so uncentered the person is not there. When family commitments are in critical condition, work can be an escape–because it is interesting and pleasurable or because my ego is being stroked or because I do not have to invest myself in intimacy. In all this, single-hearted love is really getting lost. Whether I am on a Dilbert track or a Donald Trump track, I am losing my soul. This is the time when Christ's call for change will become very insistent–because we will find ourselves in the grip of the noonday devil with its question: "Is this all there is?" We may be lamenting or hopeful or frustrated. But since we are his, Christ will not let us disengage from love–he will transform our chaos into single-heartedness. If we are willing to remain with him and acknowledge the truth, he can and will put us back together.

The successful transition is to become capable of living and giving other kinds of life–Christ's kind of life–to our world. The world of spirituality opens up significantly, as does our awareness of and desire to give God's life to the world. The gift of single-heartedness lead us to assent to God's disposition of our lives and relationships of love: we are assimilated into Christ's heart and mission. In all this, the metaphors by which we make sense of our communion with God may shift and become fluid. Our love is being stretched to become co-extensive with God's. At this point the ways of the married and the consecrated celibate converge. Also at this point those who have been living at the periphery of a committed life have a window of opportunity. There are many examples of mid-life conversions. Now there is a greater communion among those living in God's covenant of love. All our nonsense about which is the "holier" way finally can be seen as absurd and can be left behind.

Jesus' way is the way of love, the way of God's reigning in us, as we see in the Beatitudes. Because the believer has successfully integrated God's self-giving love and the pull toward the pleasurable in erotic love, there no longer needs to be tension between them–for example, *agape* can embrace the erotic, and vice versa–since they are integrated in our heart/body/spirit. However, we do need to note that Jesus is not concerned about eros–he is busy trying to help us integrate friendship and *agape*: "No one has greater love than this, to lay one's life for one's friends" (Jn 15: 13), which he reiterates in his last exchange with Peter: "Simon Peter, do you love me (will you lay down your life for me/ are you my friend)?" This is why the development of friendship that enhances the other's life is the *sine qua non* of single-hearted love in mid-life.

At mid-life, giving one's life so that others may live is the shape of singleness of heart. The form is not primarily erotic, because the work of chastity, the integration of all dimensions of the person in love, is becomimg something new, the direct work of the Spirit. In all its expressions, love is now flowing directly from God's loving, within which the believer lives. It is a gift of the Holy Spirit and the Spirit's fruit. The *CCC* understands the gifts of the Spirit to be permanent capacities to follow the promptings of the Holy Spirit (1830). Though latent in all believers, they assert themselves fully only when the virtuous life has freed the person from destructive habits of heart. At mid-life, the habit of chastity has freed the believer to love truly and broadly, as God does.

Now spirituality will begin to shift (if it has not already done so) from a sense of autonomous agency–I want to do good for others–to a deeper understanding and experience of how Jesus' infinite desire and capacity is bringing us (and through us, others) the fullness of life. We begin to see how this is brought to bear in us and flows from us to others. From this point on there need be no limit to our desire and ability to bring life to the world. For the Kingdom, which Jesus reflects on in the Beatitudes, is breaking in, full force. And the Christian whose heart has become teachable and willing is able to open to it. It is usually in mid-life that Christian singleness of heart can be seen in its mature form. Everything up till now has been a process of acquiring it, so single-hearted love has been only flowering, as it were, something we intuited. Now the fruit of chastity becomes visible in us as in Jesus and the greatest saints. And it becomes a hope for the world.

REFLECTION GUIDE

What crisis or crises precipitate the mid-life shift to integration? What has been your experience of this shift?

Why can a strong sense of self both make love possible and be an obstacle to it?

Love, mentoring, letting go are signs of single-heartedness. How are these shown in married life? In celibate life?

What is meant by saying that single-hearted chastity shifts from being a virtue to being a gift of the Holy Spirit? Why is it important that this shift happen?

Give examples of how Jesus has gradually taken over in your life and loving.

8

Mid-Life
Voices
Moira at Sixty

Even during my high-school years, when my religiosity was mainly theoretical, as my life was disorderly and self-preoccupied, God had been calling me to himself. I felt the call to consecrated life and had even applied to the teaching congregation which ran the school I attended. Then right after graduation, I fell in love with one of the boys of the group I ran around with. So when friendship with K. turned hormonal and I was smitten, my world was turned on its head. I felt loved for the first time in my life and was on fire to give myself. But in a real sense I was not all there: I had zero self-knowledge, little discipline, no sense of self-worth, plus unconscious wounds I carried from a sense of self-loathing and guilt that resulted from an episode of abuse during my childhood. My psychological salvation, such as it was, lay in my brains and sense of humor. However, true adolescent that I was, I imprudently dropped everything that had mattered to me–God, higher education, mission–to orient myself to getting married. Since nothing was going to happen until K. finished school, there was a providential delay that let things cool down. Then he broke off the engagement, and I went into a tailspin over the rejection.

I grieved awhile and gradually got my life of prayer refocused and began helping out with the parish religious-education and mission programs. I continued reading spiritual books, and the desire to give my life to the God who loved me (take that, K.!) reasserted itself, especially in a couple of retreats during which I experienced that Jesus loved me greatly and faithfully even when I was not loving him. Because of my superficial reading of popular books about happy Carmelites cheerfully going without things (I was not very deep), I felt attracted to Carmelite life. When I talked to my pastor about this, he suggested I make a retreat to think things over. He gave me a book that turned out to be the Ignatian Exercises, and I spent eight days covering the thirty-two chapters of the book. It was a time of consolation, by the end of which God made it very clear that he did not want me to be a Carmelite; he wanted me to "teach religion." I was twenty-one, and my yes to God was total–or as total as it could be when I was twenty-one.

I was accepted by a small missionary community and was fortunate to have an enlightened novice mistress. She taught me meditative prayer and provided a serious program in theology, scripture and spirituality. I came to living knowledge of God in study, in prayer, as well as to the assurance that it was this living knowledge that I had to give to others. The call to celibacy came totally clear during the first year. I had occasional bouts of rejection blues and jealousy, especially as I found out that K. had moved on and was engaged to a mutual friend. The novice mistress helped me detach myself and refocus my choices. This was when I knew with total clarity that Jesus was calling me to choose him as the only focus of my love and as my only lover and that I needed to give a complete and irrevocable yes to his call. Which I did.

But I was still very self-preoccupied. The silence of novitiate life allowed my introversion to flourish, so that I scarcely noticed people around me. I was better educated than most of the community; the sense of difference was not a problem for me, since my take on things had always been different. I was learning to serve, but was incapable of the laid-back, friendly warmth of community interaction and expectation. What they felt was that I just did not fit in, and I was not allowed to renew my vows. In those days no explanations were given. I had been there for six years and was certain that total celibate commitment was God's will for me, as I found him in prayer, ongoing learning and teaching. Nothing prepared me for this rejection except an absolute, deeply rooted certainty that God loved me and that he and I were together for the long haul. I cried most of my tears, but felt betrayed by God, angry and depressed as I went home to pick up the pieces of my life. I have never handled rejection well. I was certainly not seeing any correlation between these losses and the call to be for God-alone.

I still felt called to formal evangelization, but, in that post-Vatican II transition, the only teaching opportunities for a lay woman were in college settings. Then as conciliar documents came flowing out, with their emphasis on the role of the laity in the Church, I began advanced studies and finished with master's degrees in English and Religion. I was studying at a secular university because in those days there were no accessible Catholic theology programs that would accept women. I grew, but painfully. I had to change my approach to life and reality in a variety of situations simultaneously: from religious, back to lay life; from Aristotelian philosophy to something vaguely phenomenological; from scholastic theology to scriptural; from pre- to post-Vatican II concerns.

At the same time I was casting about for a community to help me sustain, in this radically different situation, the celibacy I had promised. God led me to a secular institute, even though I was not particularly attracted to that way of life. I stayed upset with God for about six years, during which time my prayer life was superficial and only naked faith sustained my unenthusiastic yes. I tried not to have too intimate a relationship with God, keeping him at a cool distance as much as possible, mostly because my mind was constantly being blown by all the changes in my life, and I had no energy left for God. Thinking that everything depended on me really took its toll. During retreats God consoled me greatly, though I never totally surrendered, for fear of being rejected again. I was very ambivalent–I loved God and knew he loved me, yet did not feel his love or trust his compassion. I could certainly have used a spiritual director, as I was so uptight and fearful of criticism and rejection that I was pretty closed in on myself.

The honeymoon was definitely over. God was calling, and, at one level of my soul, I was saying yes. But simultaneously I was setting limits to God's rights over me and unconsciously laying down a load of conditions. I was thirty and taking back the gift of myself penny by penny. I was feeling estranged and needed help.

The leader of the community was intelligent but exigent and she dominated community interaction with her parental leadership style. My soul began to shrivel in the situation, but I was too fearful of yet another rejection to confront the situation and search for a solution. Work was my escape and my salvation–trying to get established at the colleges, beginning adult education. Entering the highly-specialized field of theology in my thirties was difficult. I took whatever jobs I could get, sometimes working two or three free-lance jobs simultaneously to make ends meet. I enjoyed the intellectual give and take, even with college students for whom my courses were requirements to be gotten through with as little expenditure of energy as they could get away with. Work with young religious and adults was much more satisfying, as both groups were eager to learn. The adults, especially, had life experience to bring to the discussions, and so with them, as with the religious, the classes could be faith-deepening for me as well as for them. I was busy, but since I was teaching theology I was reading extensively in various areas, and class preparation was sustaining, if not intensifying, my prayer life, even though I was not completely healed of my disillusionment with God.

Then, in my late thirties, I made the thirty-day Ignatian Exercises, which transformed me and my teaching. I came to know God the Father personally through Jesus' experience and through scripture. A whole other world opened up. My prayer became much more deeply contemplative. God kept verifying his call to me and sustaining my fidelity when I felt fed up with the nonsense in Church and community (this was the early 1970s and everyone was unmoored). I was trained to give the Exercises and was incorporating the approach into my teaching, as well as offering retreats here and there.

The community situation was rapidly becoming very dysfunctional, and I became a target of scapegoating. Since I had never really learned how to deal with rejection well, I bore this as patiently as I could, but was allowing the criticism to erode what little sense of self-worth I had. Whenever I got fed up and tried to discern if it were time to leave the community, God's answer was always no. So I took my only option–to try to consciously join Jesus in his being rejected, and hang on. I did a lot of reading on the dark night of the soul and was able to make two retreats a year. Then toward the end of my thirties I had an experience of the meaning of my yes to God. Jesus told the Father: "Here she is," implying that we were engaged as equals, somehow, and that I was ready. Then the Father gave me the gift of freedom and told me that whatever I chose would be fine with him. I had been trained to suspect this kind of experience; it seemed so improbable that I could not deal with it, and simply repressed it.

During this period, I was too scattered. The pieces of my life were too separated from each other. I taught because I enjoyed it *and* because I was making God better known and loved, fifty-fifty. I worked hard at trying to help my community grow, because I felt that the grace of a call to celibacy and Christ's mission had to be responsibly lived out *and* because I hated the thought of being swamped by mediocrity, fifty-fifty. I prayed because I loved God *and* because it was my only viable refuge from the stresses of community life and trying to make a living. I began to discern the interior signs of being off track: cynicism about God's call and my inadequacy (I had interiorized the voices of rejection) and eating.

In my forties I began to come into my own. I gingerly allowed the implications of that experience of being espoused and affirmed to surface. I then had two competing voices in my soul: that of the crazy woman saying you don't amount to much and that of Jesus saying I am calling you to equality with me and greatness. I finally learned to use the second to neutralize the first, but slowly. This was a period in which my professional life took a significant turn toward administration and a much larger field of mission: I became a director of religious education. I was opening the diocesan office and establishing programs; the work was very creative; the bishop was supportive; I had wonderful co-workers; I was able to give things a shape toward the faith formation of diocesan ministers. It was a full-time job. In fact, as it developed, it became three full-time jobs. Every time I got a new idea, I could shape it and set it up. If there was no one to take up the work of implementation, I did so, feeling that having conceived it, I had to bring it to term. Basically, I was shoring up my ego to counter the voices of diminishment and was placing the relationship to God in second place in the process.

Prayer became much darker at this time, which seemed to me to be normal (according to the books), but so did the workings of my soul. I chose the way of fidelity to the work I had, but the truth is that I was not really discerning whether God wanted me to do all the things I was doing. I suspected that all was not well, but was not willing to face God's point of view directly. I saw that I was doing much good and that the fruits seemed to be great. Besides, it distracted me from the community situation, which was getting worse. This provided a clear field for desolation, and my soul became a battleground. My soul was still in pieces and I was not in touch with the full truth about myself. Since I was troubled interiorly and had no one to talk to, I began to journal; this somewhat clarified for me what God and I were really up to. The trouble was that I was so busy with work that I only plugged in to God when I was feeling really desolate. I spewed a lot of angst onto paper. This was the only clarity I got in prayer; God's reassurances came through teaching.

Since I was so over-extended at work, I became exhausted–I was well into my fifties, after all–and I began to feel the need of spiritual renewal. So I made the Spiritual Exercises for the second time. I spent thirty days wrestling with my demons: my frustrations with the community, my interiorizing of the voices of diminishment (that I now recognized as coming from a combination of others' envy of and feeling overwhelmed by my expertise–someone once compared me to a tank), my inability to make myself acceptable–plus plain exhaustion. It was a time of temptation, forcing me to examine every root of my spiritual choices and consciously discern its origin and correspondence with God's holiness which was calling me to oneness with Christ. God's voice was quiet, so I had to struggle through, drawing conclusions and making choices on my own. What helped me most during this period was continued journaling, which gave some objective shape to my experience, allowing me to look at what was going on and understand it somewhat. Even before the end of the retreat I realized that I was no longer afraid of temptation.

I suspected, and now realize, that God was strengthening me for worse to come. The community was moving toward a crisis. There were two factions: one that seemed locked in a spiritual dead end, and another that wanted to live, but needed breathing space to get their spiritual lives in order. At the end of the retreat, God gave me the choice between contemplative life and a life of action, specifically the work of trying to bring life to those in the community who wanted to live. I chose the latter because the active life had always been God's will for me in the past and because God made me realize that, at the time, I seemed the only person in the group spiritually strong enough to intervene and take action. The results of this decision were that I began to love the group, helping them by trying to strengthen them make their decisions freely and with greater faith.

Work began to expand. I and my co-workers initiated programs for the Latino community. Each expansion meant more work. Then we got a new bishop who spent money very reluctantly. By the time I was fifty-five, I was doing the work of three people and feeling oppressed by the diocesan bureaucracy. When the stress finally made me unable to sleep, it was time to leave the job. My leaving was an act of love for myself.

So in my mid-fifties, I made the change to parish work. I taught a variety of classes, all small groups. I continued trying to empower the suffering members of my community, even though this situation was beginning to make me angrier, because of injustices and what seemed general spiritual fecklessness. I began to resent demands on my time and financial resources, and reached the point of deciding that I could no longer in good conscience advise anyone to join the community. Hope in the community died. The half of the community that wanted to live their commitment in some depth received permission to become an independent group. In the discernment that went into the new identity, it became clear that, if the community were to make an impact in the new location, new strategies needed to be developed and several long-standing customs would have to be changed. The central administration was not receptive to the community's concerns, so after much soul-searching and prayer, the group gave birth to a more inclusive lay community that seemed better adapted to the realities of modern American life. With the approval of new community by the Ordinary, hope revived in me–community truly was part of my path to God.

I believe that this new direction grew directly from my willingness to wrestle with my demons during the Exercises. And my engagement with the inception of the new community was a deliberate choice to be a life giver–trying to love people enough that they could again find their center in God's call to them. However, my difficulty still lay in feeling that, since I had initiated things, I had to work to keep the groups viable. Ego dies hard. I knew, in fact, that God had done the initiating, but I took on the whole burden of ongoing growth of the group. This entailed much traveling over three counties, which seemed right, as God was calling three people to form the nucleus of a Spanish-speaking community. My sense was that if God was calling anyone to the community, he must want it to continue. I felt that I needed to take this on as my mission. The ascetical task soon became obvious: to move my point of view of what ought to be happening out from my ego as center and to allow the others to come forward to shape the communities and their futures. I slowly got better at it.

Then, shortly before retirement age, my job was terminated and I had to revisit the God-alone dimension of my call. I went a little crazy, with visions of myself as an indigent bag lady in my old age. After Christ reoriented me to trust in God's concern for me and to reflect in gratitude for being able to support myself so long, even on a church salary, I got rid of the house I could no longer afford, and took a job in a retirement center. This work did not develop into anything, but while I was there, God broke into my very dark and arid prayer, woke me up and gave me the certainty that he was calling me to chastity in the form of spousal intimacy (which had been the call forty years earlier). By now it had become much more completely incarnated in real commitment to others. What this meant for a distracted older woman was not very clear, but I knew I was in a process of renewal of prayer. I felt the need to take a sabbatical to work through what God was up to with me.

Retired, I realized that I was now free to follow old dreams. I contacted a mission society to see if they could use me. They offered me the job of spiritual director of the formation program. Still serving the mission of Christ, I feel privileged to be able to support these people who will be life-givers and love-givers in other parts of the world.

So my sixties are the time of facing retirement or semi-retirement and the limitations of aging. To the time of writing, the former has been in the forefront. Though I find myself still with many of the tasks of my sixties in hand, I am beginning to set priorities which correspond to my limits. Now working with missionary candidates and giving the Exercises, I began to think toward the future. I was entering the last phase of my life and wanted to know what God would have me do about it. So again I made a thirty-day retreat. This retreat did not turn on what work I had to do. It was about finally surrendering to God's proposal of love, his desire to couple with me, his affirmation that the time of true fruitfulness is approaching. I know it will be the fruitfulness of Christ and will be mine only because I am united with Christ. To enable me to do this, God had to heal the last remnants of fear that my wounds and sins might undo God's work. As I moved into real faith in God's power to do everything in the world and in me, I was freed to love and to trust him more completely.

So here I am, yet again, at the threshold of old age and a life of God-aloneness. But it is infinitely easier than at any other time in my life. For union means union: God can count on me in whatever he wants and I can count on him. What we do, we do together, in total transparency to each other. But this is only the beginning, God says. How it will end, who knows? But it means that God's life is flowing through me.

REFLECTION GUIDE

As you read this story, what tasks of early adulthood did Moira achieve by age forty? What tasks were left unfinished?

What choices would you have encouraged her to make differently?

Which of the metaphors found in Part III, were functioning centrally in the writer's life?

Reflecting on your own mid-life journey, what issues does Moira's experience lead you to focus on?

If you were Moira's spiritual director, what advice would you give her to grow more rapidly and surely toward single-hearted love, at this point in her life?

9

Mid-Life
Dancing with Solomon

I'M SLEEPING

The ultimate nightmare:
plea for union–
foot-dragging response to your need of me–
too late.
Then guilt
and shame that I've nowhere to go
but the sterile city streets,
to be rightly abused by those who don't care,
asking direction of those who don't know,
in terror of my loss and fearful freedom,
no way to find you.
For you're certainly not there
in my fear that I'll abuse the gift,
your promise to be present within my every choice
here
within,
in the spacious balsam beds
of my soul.
5:2

MY HEART'S AWAKE

Even in dreams I know
that you've taken possession of my soul,
though I couldn't let the truth be spoken
by me or you or anyone you sent to me.
Now, poised toward your love,
my soul mourns
the lie unmasked and bloodied
by the rage of those
faithfully guarding against the night
and trivial pursuits.
5:2

I'VE TAKEN OFF MY TUNIC

What makes me think it all depends on me
in this eternal foreplay of my soul's
treating with you in love? What mindless cramp
returning ever to the same old starting place–
that you expect of me some holy depth
that all my life's eluded me. No apt-
ness here: inanity and ego held
the pride of place. Not now. I'm left holding
the bag and thinking that there's some way I
have failed. And yet the truth is that I'm simply human and the whole damned thing's too big
for me. So cure my guilt-addiction now
and let me face my mediocrity
with equanimity and grace to laugh
amidst the angst. And then return to weep
the angry tears of longing and of loss.

5:3

HE DID NOT ANSWER

Lying again, Soledad?
Refusing to remember
how I took you to the Father?
Claiming that my choice of you
was some flightiness of mine, long past?
Are you freer now, or not?
Yes, on all counts.
It's I who am the bond, not you,
so let it go.
Go back into those caves where we met in silence.
Trust the silence and the emptiness
and trust the absence that is no absence
but my presence where as yet you cannot be.
5:6

HIS PRESENCE LIKE LEBANON

But you yourself are Lebanon,
that pungent rain-fresh forest
where I can breathe you, fearless,
even at night,
lungs expanding endlessly,
inhaling everything,
on the lost and lofty heights of Lebanon.
5:15

HIS CONVERSATION SWEETNESS

When I speak to them of you, they flock
and for a moment long for you.
And when you speak to me, I'm yours.
But when you're silent in the silence,
I fear abandonment. No more than they
do I remember that you're my where
and not some infinitely desired what.
5:16

LOINS INLAID WITH SAPPHIRES

Loins inlaid with sapphires
capturing the stars
and all the mystery
remembered in darkness
just below
the porous surface of the possible.
5:14

AWESOME WITH TROPHIES.

The souvenirs of battle hang on me everywhere,
    all those departures from the comfort
of my unsouled self, beyond the screaming ego,
    to the open sanctuary of silence.
So many years of moving beyond and beyond again
    in search of your holiness humming in my soul,
left with a miserable ego so scarred and pitted
    that it might as well be trashed.
Not tossed out, Soledad, but inlaid with the new,
    every wound a wonder
which our Spirit's wrought in you,
    making a splendor.
6:10

TURN YOUR EYES AWAY

Don't look at me so reproachfully,
as though I've done you some grave harm.
Why do you think your growth could not matter,
any more than it could not matter
if a man married a new-born.
You're an embryo, Soledad, a dawning.
Stop reproaching me for being God;
I've never reproached you for being human;
neither can be helped nor should be mourned.
I've had to live frustration, too,
and love it in you,
but I can't remove it or rush you through,
though I see you spirited into sunrise.
6:10

DANCE OF THE TWO CAMPS

But you are ready for the sword dance.
I'll put my sword into your hands
for you to learn to vanquish all the powers,
to dance them into peace,
into the life you live on Lebanon.
Face the masters everywhere—
in you, in them—
who will not let you grow.
Face them fearlessly, for they can't withstand
my power in you, yours in me.
It's the final choice, Soledad,
beyond all fear,
into perfect love.
6:13

LIKE TOWERING LEBANON

Let go the myth of the little lost soul:
my love's irresistibly pulling you to rise,
towering tall, straight—
in the dignity you've become—
able to embrace my coming to you in love
and to endure becoming love
to those who've long protected themselves
against the danger of your ego power and rage.
Arise, Soledad, my love.
7:4

REFLECTION GUIDE

The first four poems deal with the lies we tell ourselves in order not to acknowledge God's love in our lives. What are the lies by which you evade God's love? What are the psychic wounds such lies come from?

In His Conversation Sweetness *Soledad Marinera reflects on awareness of how life flows from the love of God. What has been your experience of this?*

Awesome with Trophies *reflects on the relation between our woundedness and God's love. What are the wounds in you that God has inlaid with jewels?*

In Dance of the Two Camps *and* Like Towering Lebanon *God asserts that he is empowering us to love as he does. Have you experienced this? Explain.*

10

Full Maturity
Unmasked, Disarmed and Wholed

Some psychologists point out that adult development is a drive to integration, by which I think they mean the discovery of who we really have become and what the meaning of our life is. The task of engaged mid-life followers of Christ is to actually become what we have been called by God to be. Gradually we moved beyond the roles we assumed in our attempts to love, and beyond their corresponding masks. We gradually (sometimes very gradually) surrendered the attitudes and behavior that either defended us from the potential dangers to the body-spirit integration of love that we thought others or God posed or the real refusal of integration we still clung to. How did such a change occur? By modeling ourselves on Jesus, who kept asserting that there was a way of gaining our lives/spirits by losing them.

In our seventies and eighties, singleness of heart should be substantially achieved—and more and more obviously as the result of God's gift.

Early on in his mission, Jesus confronted the misconceptions of the scribes and Pharisees about ceremonial cleanness and insisted that the only thing that could make a person unfit for union with God was what came from within his heart. Then he listed attitudes and behavior that flow from an adulterous heart: wicked designs, fornication, theft, murder, adultery, greed, malice, deceit, sensuality, envy, blasphemy, arrogance. But he saved the worst for last: an obtuse spirit (Mark 7). A consciousness–a heart–that has not become single and transparent becomes blunted, blurred. And when this lack of perception is about ourselves and our relationship with God, it can be death-dealing, for it makes us truly heartless. If, when I am old and looking toward the future, I do not know myself truly loved and loving, united with a beloved God, in communion with other loved and loving people, where else can I go, except into despair?

But mature Christians do know, and the fruit of single-hearted love includes joy and peace, and much more (Gal 5: 22). The battle for self-discipline and the struggle to love amid the wild variety of people and situations that life brought us, now pay off. God moves us to become ourselves and we can leave our masks behind, along with the lies they represent. We become our true selves. But then, in full maturity, the shadow side of the body-spirit integration appears. The body that has carried love forward and given a skin to God's love in the world now begins to fall away, disintegrate, as it were. Not just in the cosmetic signs of aging, but in the malfunctions, small and great, from constipation to cancer, which begin to define our mortality. What singleness of heart now does is to help us redefine mortality as eternal life, life in its fullness as it is in God.

The person who is living totally by Christ's Spirit no longer has to divide his life into bytes of conscious intention and choice, no longer thinks that who he has become is based on limited human power to either create or destroy. There is no blunting of love or the consciousness of being loved by God or of loving God and others. There is only openness to the world of loving, the Trinitarian world. The irony is that the fullness of life is now expressed in the limits of aging and decline in the strength of our physical or mental faculties. Our memory may not always be functioning well, nor imagination, nor reason. The books that try to describe the dark night of the soul in union with God are unanimous in saying that the darkness in these areas is the result of the fullness of light in the deepest reaches of the soul, where light is sheer love. As old age begins, we try to fight off all loss of function and maintain autonomy and control. But ultimately we are not in control of the final integration of everything in love– that is the Spirit's work–and so we eventually surrender to it. In those whose faculties are still functioning normally, the fruit is joy, light-heartedness and freedom to engage others directly, without pretence or pretension. Such people become transparent to the Spirit in them. In those whose abilities are lessening, there remains only who they are in God–as we observe in some old people diagnosed with dementia. What we can see from the sidelines is only partial. They may be clinically demented, violent, unresponsive or hostile, but they are not necessarily biblically de-hearted. They are simply in the hands of God's love, there where they have lived and found their home. For all, then, death is a simple transition into a love without limits, that love at the deepest center of our soul.

Does this means that old age is the end of ability to move out to others so that they may have life? Not if we are impelled by Christ's Spirit in everything. For as long as the Spirit continues to breathe and act in the depths of the soul, life radiates from mature Christians without their having to choose that it happen. At times in his life Jesus suddenly became aware that power had gone out from him, without his knowledge or choice (Mark 5: 30). The Spirit, in whose communion he lived, chose. And so, through mature Christians, the life of Christ overflows into the world. This is the dimension of single-heartedness that our contemplative nuns and monks understand and commit themselves to, and the rest of us finally come to live: Jesus healing and wholeing the world through us because we are joined to him and embody his life wherever we are–in a hermitage, in service, in a long-term nursing facility. And after death, everywhere.

REFLECTION GUIDE

Why does the failure to become single-hearted and loving lead to despair?

What are the masks that are still being worn by you (or by someone close to you) as you approach seventy (or more): What grace would you ask from God to help you/him remove them?

Who is the most life-giving old person you know? Describe her impact on you.

Why is the diminishment of aging and death not an obstacle to giving life to the world? Give examples from your experience.

To love and let go of how this love is extended is the Spirit's gift to the aged. Do you know anyone who does this? What are the signs that this work is in progress?

11

Full Maturity
Voices
Corazón at 90

How did a child born shortly after World War I, in a southern city of many cultures, with the cruelty of segregation, and dominance of a mixture of Catholic traditions and the celebration of Pan, Dionysius, Venus–how did I choose religious life and its celibacy? All I thought I wanted was a passionate, indulgent human lover. How did I come to consecrated celibacy and "the only Thou who makes all life worthwhile," as William Barry phrased it? I was never attracted to religious life as work or community. Secretly, I felt scornful of women religious who rhapsodized about "leaving the world." I loved my world, was fiercely attached to it, and never left it. As I write the story of how God loved me into my present joy as a vowed celibate, I see that only God could have extricated me from the contradictions between the life I chose and the impulses, images and the feelings that were at home in my consciousness until I reached genuine old age. I am the proof that God loves us so completely that he never gives up looking for any way at all to bring us to union with himself.

Between the ages of one and four, things happened which I remember as casting a persistent shadow over my life. First, the sense that my mother was not completely accepted by my father's family. I knew my parents were very much in love when they married but I saw they were entirely different in personality and preferences; they quarreled often until I was about eight, and the quarreling always sent me into a quagmire of fear and sadness–fear of abandonment, a strange wrenching pity for them both and wild grief at the prospect of losing either. The images faded with the quarrels but my body persisted in remembering; a vague and sometimes piercing and terrifying fear haunted my life–and perhaps set off later destructive choices. However, the other side of this was that I was the bearer of a proud family name and was passionately loved by my favorite aunt and by my father, who responded to the sniping of another aunt: "How can I grieve that I have no son when I have this beautiful little girl?" From these experiences came a profound sense of entitlement. This became the source of my discounting others and imposing myself on them, which was coupled with the belief that they could not really love me if they became aware of my deceptiveness. I felt that I was only pretending to be interested and involved with others–when all I wanted, or thought I wanted, was to be alone. However, over time I began to see that my quick tiring with others was not a thirst for solitude but a desire to be doing something more interesting to myself, like reading.

By the time I was six I found I could read whatever I picked up; I read voraciously. However I never confused the stories from Scripture with the numerous tales from Greek and Roman mythology, my earliest books. Except for Jesus, I found mythology much more exciting than the Bible. I made up ongoing tales about myself and Pluto, riding away to the mysterious underworld! These daydreams began very early and, with altering images, formed the major part of my escape route from whatever seemed merely tiresome or unpleasant or a dark reality was upon me. Once I transformed a story I had daydreamed into criticism of an innocent relative, releasing a storm in the family. For me, the lesson was: *never* tell anyone what is going on inside, and this determination brought me to live–consciously and subconsciously–in several unrelated worlds.

Another, much smaller and less pervasive–blessed be God–element of my escape route would shadow my life darkly into old age. When I was about four, I discovered self-pleasuring. I do not know how. I was excited, intrigued and ashamed when I discovered I could make it happen.

Both parents were very devout Roman Catholics. We said the rosary together nightly. However, the things said by my teachers about our Lady's absolute perfection made me feel uncomfortable with her. I was certain she disapproved of my daydreams and even more of the masturbation which I indulged in when I felt unsure or out of place in any situation. However, the point of faith that mattered and matters enormously to me today is that Jesus–the real risen Jesus–is really present in the sacred host kept in the tabernacle. I do not remember ever *not* knowing this. I never asked how he could be there. To me the truth was obvious: Because he is God he was able to be there, alive, listening, always there, real, sublimely happy. At my first communion I felt an immense sense of having arrived. I knelt quietly and said to our Lord: "Thank you for coming to me. When I grow up I will be a sister. For now, I want to daydream." I did not know I was choosing a life of misery, opening myself to contradictions that only God could and would resolve.

As I was beginning my last two years of grammar school, preparing for confirmation, I was blessed with an excellent teacher who knew how to foster love for our Lord in children. She noticed that during recess I would ask permission to visit the Blessed Sacrament in the adjacent church. I loved to go into that quiet place to daydream. This allowed me an approved escape from the rough sports of the playground, which, as a child small for her age, I hated. One day Sr. R. handed me a little booklet: "When you go to church, you might like to use this." It was titled *A Child's Visit with the Blessed Sacrament.* I eagerly accepted the booklet which became for me an introduction to talking with God directly in my own language, and I used it through high school. The same teacher invited our class to come to Holy Mass each Saturday in honor of Our Lady. Doing this made me more comfortable with Mary; besides, I loved the deep silence of the near-empty church and was buoyed up for the day by a sense of our Lord's presence. However, my introduction to the Eucharist as a community action of the entire Mystical Body, the worshipping community, came about in an entirely different way. In my parish church I always felt alone with God. Then my father introduced me to the adventure of early Saturday morning Mass, an hour's streetcar ride from our house, in an ornate church packed with enthusiastic devotees of our Lady of Perpetual Help, alive with song and joyously shared cries to our Lady. This experience, Saturday after Saturday when I was eleven, opened my soul permanently to the wonder of actually belonging to the people of God.

Grade school had been unchallenging. High school was different! My teachers were excellent, homework was mostly essays on current topics, history and literature—and my school taught four years of Latin. My religion teacher spoke easily of God; our religion text was superb—it really explained holy Mass. The school chaplain gave excellent lectures once a week. Then for my thirteenth birthday my parents gave me a daily missal, so I now followed the text word for word, intently, in Latin and English. One day, after a year of Latin, I noticed the prayer: "Grant that through the mystery of this water and wine we may become partakers of his divinity who humbled himself to share our humanity." The Latin for partakers was *consortes* (by that time I had a feeling for what Latin meant). Consorts! Much more than partakers! Queens were consorts—sallying forth hand-in-hand with the King! Suddenly *I knew grace was not a thing*. Grace was God's life, was God. I would really become like God. I was stunned. I received Holy Communion in a dazzle of joy. That was the beginning of a love for the sacraments that has grown and is perhaps the primary reason why I could never leave the Catholic Church.

I had joined a vocation club, an inquiry group about religious life. Then I discovered that the Mother Superior intended to send me away to college the moment I finished the obligatory two-year canonical training. "Your daughter will never have to do any housework," she said soothingly to my mother. "Not Corazón. She is going to school!" At that moment I knew I could never enter that particular convent. I had seen the way some of the teachers scolded the domestic sisters. It made me cry in anger and pity–it was so unfair! I did not want to be a part of that elite. Besides, I wanted my going to the convent to be a gift to God. I passionately wanted college but had decided to go to the convent instead. If college was guaranteed, as I assumed from the superior's comment, what had I to give? Weird reasoning–but it set me looking for another community to replace that of my good teachers.

The sisters had persuaded my reluctant mother to let me board at the school during my junior year. I wanted to, as a kind of adventure, but that fast went sour. I did not know how to get myself back home. In October I began to read continuously, day and night, sleeping scarcely at all and eating poorly. Fortunately for my mental and physical health, a state of blinding eye strain developed. I was forbidden to read at all and, happily, my mother insisted that I return home. One day my father asked: "Now that you have time, why not go to daily Mass?" So I did. After my eyes healed sufficiently, I wanted to explore what my *Following of Christ* had to say about mental prayer. *Following* said too much, and I gradually learned to simplify the process so that thinking about God and talking to him, rather than preliminary acts, took up most of the time. This old classic had been my father's graduation present when I completed grammar school.

God himself then gave me a greater gift during my year of not reading. This was a Christmas retreat preached by a young, brilliant teacher who had studied spirituality in Rome. His topic was the Beatific Vision. "Faith becomes light; we no longer think ideas about God–but God becomes our thought; as now, we in a way become what we think or feel intensely–so then we actually, really become–God! So intensely are we with God that our consciousness is God's consciousness… with all God's joy, beauty, truth, goodness that is the eternal God…the dance of Father, Word, Spirit is our dance." I *felt* what he was trying to say. I began to try to see how anything I did could be done "in order to get to God." But when prayer was dry and I felt nothing, I day-dreamed and masturbated. Years would pass before I truly understood and accepted the incompatibility between these romantic/erotic daydreams of adventures with Pluto, who gradually became an identifiable human lover, and true, lasting intimacy with God. I constantly resolved and constantly failed to change my behavior. This left me in a chronic state of unrest.

Meanwhile I continued to seek a personally meaningful response to the question: why am I on earth? The catechism's answer left me cold. I found what I needed in G. K. Chesterton's life of Thomas Aquinas: "The purpose of life is the praise of God as the author of life and being." What struck me was that praise and happiness went together. I suddenly felt that God made me for happiness and that this happiness had somehow to come from God. The sky opened! This sentence has been the lodestar that, until this day, keeps me sane and moving somehow into God despite the fears, falls and follies of my daily life. I knew then that I had to find for myself the kind of life in which I could best praise the God of all existence, and I knew clearly that I could not do it alone. I needed a one-goal, one-track life that offered the support of other like-minded persons on a similar quest. Through a friend of the family I found what I needed: a new group of simply-clad sisters, young, friendly, who worked along the muddy roads and tiny farms of several Southern states–where education was minimal, health care rare and soul care almost non-existent. These sisters served according to what circumstances demanded as catechists, nurses, social workers, mediators. My life's main task was clear! God was the point of their life, the meaning. I would join them and find happiness!

I was determined to do this directly upon graduating from high school. My mother was adamant in her no, and at seventeen I was not free to enter without parental permission. I decided then to give my mother a year of doing what she wanted me to, and once I was eighteen, I would simply walk out. The thought of doing this caused floods of tears: I loved my mother with a protective tenderness but felt I had to begin my life's work. Then, six months after graduation, a second, brief, eye-opening event occurred. I had refused a college scholarship, both from fear of losing my vocation to a life of academia and because the new community's charming but somewhat unrealistic foundress assured me I needed no more than my excellent high-school training. With the happy approval of my mother, I eagerly attended any free educational event I could find. Innocently, I went to a meeting of the American Catholic Philosophical Association. The paper I heard (but understood none of) was couched in technical thomistic language. It was the first time in my life that I had heard something I did not immediately understand. I was devastated. Almost blind with a kind of sick despair, I stumbled into our parish church. I stood weeping before Jesus in the empty church: "What crazy mistake have I made, O my God, in refusing the scholarship? How can my ignorance serve you? Have I permanently crippled myself to be of any use to you? How will I explain you to your people?" Suddenly I felt he was regarding me with compassionate love. I burst out: "You know I did it for you! You know that you let me do it. All right! I count on you to let me know what I need to know to teach about you." Immediately, calm came. What I knew is that God is trustworthy. Absolutely. He would see that I had what I needed. Yes. I am the one who cannot be trusted. Not him. Through my worst failures against him, God has never abandoned me. God has always given me what I needed. God's trustworthiness is a fact I cannot *not* die for. I think I am almost ontologically incapable of denying it, so consistent is God's goodness. Despite this, I have treated him terribly. But this conviction at the center of my soul, that God would never refuse to give me what I need to serve him, never left me and often saved my sanity and my soul.

The following spring I read Catherine of Siena's life and tried briefly to model myself on her. One day, bored by hours of baking, I allowed myself to fall into daydreams, more adventures with Apollo and Pluto. I felt guilty but belligerent, and carefully avoided evaluating these daydreams. I only knew in some sad, dim, sharply humiliated, guilty-heart-sinking way that I had missed an open door and that, thereafter, mine would be a long, wretched way home. Gone was any ease I had briefly enjoyed in ridding myself of daydreams. I struggled against them, resolving day after day, week after week, year after year, not to daydream. But suddenly some chance image or vivid remark would trigger my imagination. I noticed finally that this seemed to happen in situations where I felt in some way marginal. I was escaping into an imaginary place far away where I was the center of attention. The daydreams did not come alone. The lure of self-pleasuring slipped in, persisted. I never kept a single resolution. I could never win any skirmish or battle. Though I read Freud's theory that daydreams and often resultant masturbation are normally grown out of, have little to do with morality and are not to be brooded about—in my case, not so. I was filled with guilt, fear, self-loathing, but both attachments persisted. I yearned to be free and my prayers had turned to mute, nearly hopeless pleading. God would answer me in his mercy, not because of any resolution kept on my part.

But let us go back to then. Summer arrived; my mother met the sisters, was charmed, and two months later, before I was nineteen, I entered the community. Now I tried to live my two lives simultaneously—the deliberate search for union with God, and the other self-preoccupied and intensely self-absorbed life of the imagination. A convent is not a place where a person is likely to be the center of attention. I plunged into the prayer, study and contemplation of the early years of formation. I had the opportunity not only of going to college but of earning a Ph.D. in theology. I loved the years of my twenties and early thirties, as I felt my soul expand into the combined worlds of theology and love of God. My daydreams decreased significantly because I was so interested in my studies, but the masturbation continued. During all those years I was never straightforward with my confessors about the split between what I was doing and what I was deeply desiring to be. What was and has remained my salvation is that I never abandoned prayer. I would spend time before the Blessed Sacrament, in dryness, mostly reading, in order to keep my attention on God, and always with a sense of God's kindness to me. But I never conceived, much less tried to implement any plan to reform.

I was appointed novice director in my early thirties. I set out to create the perfect novitiate for the members in formation, a process that would combine intense development of their relationship with God in prayer with solid theological teaching, appreciation of all the arts, realistic practice in living life in community, and engaging in the community's mission. As new members entered who could respond to all these dimensions and I discovered among the novices a highly talented kindred spirit, my dreams began to include the desire that my vision be perpetuated,. I worked to impose my plan on the community, yet another egotistic "time-bound pleasure," from which God was trying to free me. The community reacted against the spirit of this project, I think: instead of pinning it on God I was pinning it on successors molded into my own image. The anointed successor was sent away. The dream was dead. I was forty-three that month.

    The collapse of the dream sent me into sixteen years of bitterness and anger at the superiors whom I felt had robbed me of the great creative formation plan I alone, with my now-gone ally, could have created in our group for years to come. My anger had led me almost to despise the whole community, to distance myself from my amazingly patient, loving sisters. I neglected communal happenings, immersing myself in outside concerns: teaching, working intensely with a council of all the religious women in the area, pursuing all available cultural events. I also immersed myself in sensuality: I entered into an unhealthy three-year lesbian relationship. Masturbation continued. If I could have found a good excuse to leave the convent, I would have. So I left psychologically. In some complex way I do not understand, after a total of ten years, our Lord's words, "Father forgive them; they know not what they do," melted and converted my judgmental heart. Doubtless it was the prayer and consistent compassion of my unusually just, yet merciful, superior that saved me, guided and supported me in my saner and wiser movements and decisions. Not once during this ten years did this good woman ever act as if I were wicked and hopelessly lost, though I myself often felt so. God enabled me to let go entirely of my anger and bitterness. I was too ashamed to face my sisters and tell them I had been wrong; nor did I use this grace to reorient myself to God; in fact, I avoided finding a spiritual director, in spite of being a spiritual guide for others. It never occurred to me that I needed to make any reparation for my infidelity to God. I was now fifty-nine, a presumptive time of wisdom—but not for me.

Six years passed in a kind of dreary, uneasy peace. Prayer had become study. Then boredom precipitated a second lesbian relationship. I felt dominated, profoundly guilty, caught yet longing for freedom. I longed to be free of it; I pleaded with God to free me, but I was too cowardly to take responsibility for ending the relationship. Of course, I never spoke to any confessor or spiritual director (except by extreme indirection). I was spending all possible time with this woman, satisfying my craving for the new and interesting by traveling. After passionate nights together, I felt that the relationship was sucking all the life out of me. This made me cling more desperately to prayer and Holy Mass—but my heart was fragmented. I did do good things: my work as director, together with teaching and working with justice groups with the poor filled my days. In my late sixties I helped care for my mother through her final illness. Then, within a year, one sister died— followed shortly by my youngest sister, whom I nursed until her peaceful death. I was fiercely repressing all emotion through all this and closing my ears to God's call to seek my joy in him alone. I collapsed with cancer in my early seventies. Only the certainty of my death from the cancer gave me the courage to listen to the Lord's voice as he repeated the Father's loving admonition to Cain: you can choose. These words gave me the palpable support I needed, and I ended the life-sucking relationship. The daydreams were now gone, but not the occasional compulsion to seek physical self-pleasure.

Then began ten years of relative peace. Nothing extraordinary: I ended academic teaching, taught adult groups, wrote letters, did spiritual direction, traveled. However, I never really set about changing myself. During this period my addiction to masturbation continued; my daily hour of prayer was mostly a cry for mercy. God was in process of doing everything—while I was simply the object of his mercy.

Early in my eighties I was plunged into six years of almost unbroken anxiety and terror, with dreams of endings, lostness, and dusty, cobwebby, dilapidated rooms. Only daily holy Mass and communion–always a moment of hope and trust– preserved my sanity. Driven by near despair, I sought help in a residential program for religious in crisis, where another stage of my conversion took place. I was fortunate to be able to get the psychological help I needed and serious spiritual direction. Finally, God the Father embraced me with his presence and said: "Yes. Time-bound pleasure does last only a few seconds…a brief poor shadow of eternal joy. You know now why it was and is so insistent." Those words entirely and permanently freed me from my addiction to any sort of self-pleasuring. I was eighty-eight.

The dry bones of my soul began to reassemble. In the context of the program, I was also freed from my greatest obstacle to loving–discounting people. What I now began to see, thanks to group therapy, was the healing that comes through consistent respect and real concern. God so healed me of discounting people that from then on I did not want to criticize people or hear them criticized. I stopped judging and began to accept that "circumstances are the humble messengers of God's providence," as Martin Gillet puts it. The final words of the program director in my admission interview had been: "Sister, the word is surrender! Surrender, Sister, surrender!" My immediate reaction was a rush of anger–then fear–then enormous relief that almost brought tears. These words, expanded by some paragraphs of Benedict XVI on acceptance and receiving as the primary maturing agents of creaturehood, focused my attention on the importance of living in the now. Acceptance became a moment-by-moment seeing the various circumstances of my life as either invitations or cautions from God about how I should use my time. Receiving became accepting with a glance of gratitude to God the compliments, small gifts and pleasure I frequently received from others. Formerly such things filled me with uneasy, frantic denial of my worthiness. I now began to know clearly that indeed I am not worthy but need to be humbly grateful for these signs of God's goodness. What began to fill me was the awareness of God's exquisite mercy. As a result, I am taking ever more seriously our Lord's one command and one prohibition: the command to love one another and the prohibition "judge not." This determined attitude is transforming my life

However, there remain mood swings between anxiety and radiant peace, but with total freedom from addiction to any sort of self-pleasuring. Though I am steadfastly unwilling to judge or criticize others, I am plagued by flashes of feeling myself better than they are. Nothing good that I do seems untinged by some defect or other. I was still undergoing bouts of darkness and fear of God as some kind of monster.

A few months ago I suffered a fourth bout of congestive heart failure, during which I felt myself totally surrounded by a sea of the light of God's presence. I did not fear dying; rather I longed to float out on that radiant water over which God was coming toward me. Two days later, I was alive and being discharged from the hospital. But I was no longer the person who entered there five days earlier. I was terribly disappointed to be alive. After three days of intense disorientation I realized I was going to get well, and, in the face of this, God gave me the grace to tell him I wanted only to do his will. Almost at once I received yet another wholly unexpected gift. I must confess that for many years I have felt a coolness and disappointment with the decisions coming from the Church's magisterium in Rome. I had withdrawn my trust from the papacy, had downplayed the Church teaching about various moral and disciplinary matters. On the feast of St. Peter's Chair, I was filled with a sense of compunction for my arrogance and recalled vividly the words of the great Benedictine, Columba Marmion, on the scripture that only the obedient man speaks of victory. I saw clearly that I had never taken seriously the Church's teaching about the disorder of homosexual activity and other expressions of unchastity; I had never challenged my homosexual directees, much less myself. I began to appreciate the importance of holding to the truth even while being compassionate with people's deep woundedness, negativity and fear, and, above all, their deep desire to love and be loved.

This is a terrible story of human weakness, blindness, failure, but it is primarily meant as a clear witness to God's most breathtakingly persistent love and mercy. Here in the last stage of my life, God has brought me to what I have always truly wanted, union with him alone. In spite of myself. All the spiritual writers tell us that we have to open our hearts so that God can enter. But not in my case. My heart was firmly closed and it has taken God more than ninety years to open it. My only contribution has been to hang on to him out of sheer necessity in desperate, never-abandoned, time for prayer. To crown his mercy he has sent me to a health-care center where a holy confessor, after each celebration of the sacrament of reconciliation, assures me, "Your sins are forgiven. Go in the peace and joy of your Lord." He is my Lord now, really and at last. And I can begin to sing in the words of Rabindranath Tagore:

> *Take, oh take! has now become my cry.*
> *scatter all from this beggar's bowl:*
> *put out the lamp of this importunate watcher;*
> *hold my hands, raise me from the still-gathering heap*
> *of your gifts*
> *into the bare infinity of your uncrowded presence.*

REFLECTION GUIDE

A lifelong struggle with masturbation was rooted in Corazón's divided heart. What were the attitudes that underlay her difficulties?

As Corazón moved into midlife she obviously did a great deal of good. Why was this not enough to mask her sense of being off track?

How did the fact of her call to celibacy both worsen her struggle and get her out of it?

Have you experienced a disconnection between what your following of Christ calls you to and what you are willing to surrender? Describe it, including God's role in it.

How did the limitations of illness help refocus Corazón's priorities?

At what point in the story did you see that single-heartedness was being achieved? What was God's role in this integration?

How would a stronger sense of community have helped Corazon to single-heartedness?

12

Full Maturity
Dancing with Solomon–At Rest

I AM MY LOVE'S

I am yours
where the snows and rains of Lebanon
water the valleys,
and the tender roots of those who long
for your love
rejoice at last.
7:10

NEW THINGS AND OLD

So long a courtship
leaving my soul
patined like antique silver
or, like ancient ivory, bloodied,
seasoned into wisdom
approaching naiveté
and new every morning,
springing into love.
7:13

DO NOT FORCE LOVE, 3

Search for me, Soledad,
only in your soul's soul
where you'll find us one,
honey flowing from the rock.
8:4

SET ME AS A SIGNET

For where you choose to love,
Soledad,
I go with you, with all my Spirit's power
in the peaceful holiness of your choice
and mine.
Just bind me to your heart.
Then in this double-driven choice of love,
the Father's gift,
death is everywhere annulled.
8:6

REFLECTION GUIDE

I Am My Love's *uses the scriptural image of water as a symbol of the Holy Spirit in us. What "tender roots" of yours are still searching for the water?*

At this time in your life how would you describe your union with God? What image predominates?

In Set Me as a Signet *God says that "death is everywhere annulled." How is death being annulled in you? What role are your choices playing in this? What role is God's choice playing in it?*

III

THE MYSTERY AND METAPHORS OF SINGLE-HEARTEDNESS

INTRODUCTION

Spirituality is the interaction of God's initiative and our response. For Christians this interaction is rooted in Jesus himself–he person in whom God made himself human and whose love embraced the Father in a totally human way. Jesus gathers us all into this relatedness–we know the Father because Jesus, the closest to the Father's heart, reveals him. Because God is infinite, this revelation will be multifaceted. But how can we know an infinite person whose reality lies beyond concepts or images? How did Jesus know God? He knew because he experienced in the depths of his heart, in his very being, and from his experience analogies surfaced in the form of metaphors.

The power of metaphor lies in the imagination's ability to fuse two dimensions of our experience of following Christ, experiences which we live at the deepest level of our souls. Metaphors are lasers that cut through logic and day to day experiences, straight to the heart, that holy place where the Spirit touches us immediately and moves us. "The Reign of God is like" was how Jesus put it widely, thus inciting us into dimensions of his own experience of single-hearted love of the Father. For Christians, our most profound experience is encountering God the Father in Jesus at the deepest center of our souls. This experience, which is wordless and non-emotional, needs to permeate our souls and attach itself to other experience of relatedness, feeling and history. The metaphor grows from this fusion. Unless they are dead, metaphors help us get in touch with this reality. Intended as a way to touch into our experience–to speak the unspeakable–they invite us to explore our relationship more deeply and may shift in meaning. However, sometimes we use them simply because our religious milieu does, without any personal experience to bring to them. Then they are simply meaningless, "zombie words," in Flannery

O'Connor's memorable phrase. Sometimes as we go deeper into our experience of God, the metaphor that once allowed us to touch the experience gets diaphanous; the surprising concreteness of it wears off, and we are left with naked truth beyond imagination. If this does not lead into silent contemplation, it will cease to be experienced on a regular basis, and will open up only now and then in our lives, when this Spirit helps us touch down into this mystery. Or we may simply forget what it means altogether.

The metaphors explored in this book fuse the incomprehensibility of God's loving offer of himself in the person of Jesus and our human struggle to love and be loved in a way that is a response to this unparalleled love. Every Christian is called to single-hearted love. Each person brings his or her own history to this call; Jesus engages each one according to his own choice of the mission of each. Therefore a person will usually be drawn more strongly by one metaphor than by another. Any given metaphor may be more or less significant at different stages in our life, as our experience of God's Spirit impelling us shifts and deepens. Clearly, then, love and intimacy, if they matter to us, demand progressive insight or grace. Jesus takes on the process and gives us his Spirit so that the metaphor will express a living experience of going deeper into the mystery of God's love and exploring the interaction between God and ourselves in new ways.

In this section of the book we will reflect on six biblical paradigms of single-hearted love: friendship, brotherhood, marriage and community, eunuchs for the Kingdom, bride of Christ, bridegroom of the Church. While each has its own distinctness, we need to note again that they are neither mutually exclusive nor gender-biased. Bride of Christ and bridegroom of the Church, for example, are two facets of a single spiritual relationship: the giving and receiving of loving and being loved. We hope to see how our growth in chastity is a progressive integration of all these elements into our relationship with Christ. The purpose of these reflections, therefore, is to help us enter more deeply into the mystery–into what God in Jesus is doing in opening the path to love in each person, the possibilities that the Holy Spirit offers those who accept the great gift of his single-hearted love. In acknowledging and living out of all these dimensions of Christian spirituality, which is, at heart, nothing but love, we will be drawn ever deeper into the mystery of our God, who is sheer loving and, seeing him as he is become like him (1 Jn 3: 2).

13

I Have Called You Friends

No one has greater love than this, to lay down one's life for one's friends. You are my friends if you do what I command you. I do not call you servants [slaves] any longer, because the servant does not know what the master is doing; but I have called you friends, because I have made known to you everything that I have heard from my Father. You did not choose me but I chose you. And I appointed you to go and bear fruit, fruit that will last, so that the Father will give you whatever you ask him in my name. I am giving you these commands so that you may love one another (John 15: 12-17).

"Friendship" is one of the "zombie words" of our culture, covering as it does the hordes of "intimate" associates of the more extraverted among us, through business associates, drinking buddies, people we went to school with. However Christian friendship has more deeply personal connotations, many of which we see in the story of Jonathan and David in 1 Samuel 18-20 and 2 Samuel 1, in which "the soul of Jonathan was knit to the soul of David, because he loved him as his own soul." In scripture, "soul" indicated the person's life force. Jonathan's life was to enhance that of David; there was nothing Jonathan would not do for David: with affection, he shared all he had with him, he went out adventuring with him, he protected him from Saul–and David tried to do the same for him. And in the end, David grieved over Jonathan: "I am distressed for you, my brother Jonathan; very pleasant have you been to me; your love to me was wonderful, passing the love of women." Friends are those whose souls, whose lives, whose very selves are forged into an inextricable oneness. So, what relationship, what degree of interweaving of Jesus' soul and our is implied when he proclaims that he and we are friends

Friendship is a mystery. What is the intuition that sees beyond the usual barriers we raise against being known and giving ourselves in such a way? What is the attraction that allows us to find our "souls" affirmed and expanded by another person, so that at any given moment that other person is the horizon against which we define ourselves. A horizon that is never not there because it is part of who we are, no matter what the distance or length of actual physical separation. A horizon that feels like home. And what is that further step into remaining faithful to the intuition of oneness that loves to the end? For all of this is part and parcel of the relationship that Jesus has for us and into which he calls us.

In the section on the developmental issues regarding chastity, we noted in passing that friendship seems to be the basic model within which Jesus was working. While he was exercising his role as healer and teacher, this relationship was perhaps obscured. But in the passage cited in the epigraph, part of his conversation with his disciples at the last supper, Jesus finally gathered them (and us) into the fullness of the mystery of his love for them and theirs for him. Jesus used the bridegroom metaphor only twice–in the context of the inbreaking of the Kingdom and the irrelevance of fasting (Mk 2:19) and in the context of his going to prepare a place for them (Jn 14:3). But here, at the end, he is gathering them, and with them, us, into the mystery of his final insight about love and relationship– friendship.

A problem we Americans have is to get beyond the debased approach to friendship we see in the innumerable sitcoms that clutter our cables and satellites. Nearly always we are presented with friendships cut off not only from the God dimension of life, but from the real life of our souls. So we need to return to the center represented by Christ. We may be tempted to think of a friend as simply a person who will not judge me or my choices, who will stand by me even as destroy myself–lose my soul. Or we may confuse friendship with eros, as in the friends-with-benefits model. Wrong turns aside, the drive to friendship is a sign that we are seeking a more enhanced human experience than is to be found in in the self-absorbed passion of eros alone. Even our tortoise-like Church has finally shifted the prerequisites for marriage in Christ to friendship and intimacy–with the emphasis on communication and shared interests and values in marriage preparation. Although, to be truthful, sometimes Jesus is left out of the discussion.

Things can go wrong with friendships, we know. What goes wrong lies in a complex of self-serving attitudes and behavior that have traditionally been called vices: innumerable variations on envy, anger, greed, apathy, lust, cowardice, arrogance. For friendship to thrive we must be aware of how such vices are showing up in our souls and take every prudent means to discipline and move beyond our base impulses. Then we will be able to accept the love that is offered us without contaminating it and offer love that enhances the friend's life without any undercurrent of self serving. As we have seen above, this is pretty much the work of a lifetime, and the dynamics will be the same for both married and unmarried people.

Our attempts at real friendship, therefore, are always slightly off, contaminated. Yet in spite of our limitations and sins, Jesus calls us his friends. What, then, are the constitutive elements of single-hearted friendship into which he is calling us? In the epigraph Jesus alludes to four:

- You are my friends if you do what I command you;
- I have called you friends, for all that I have heard from my Father I have made known to you;
- You did not choose me, but I chose you and appointed you that you should go and bear fruit and that your fruit should abide;

- The greatest expression of love is to lay down your life for your friends.

To be a friend of Jesus and in Jesus, therefore, is to live his single-heartedness in all the dimensions of God's desires, his gifts, his mission and his self-giving.

Follow my wishes–live toward the Father as I do–is Jesus' last will and testament. They were also the last words of Moses, the *shema* (Dt 6), the heart of Judaism: to hold God's covenant of love by obedience to the law of love–that is, in the heart–to express, implement, live it. Throughout the gospel we see that Jesus was constantly challenging those around him to embrace God's commands more holistically: to get beyond the dead fragments of the letter into the heart and spirit of God. And here Jesus finally summarized what this means: *agape*. To care for God and neighbor is to love, to freely lay down one's life for people's good. The greatest commandment is to love God whole-heartedly and to love the neighbor as one's very self within this love of God. The friend of God loves him single-heartedly–heart, soul, mind, spirit–and with all her physical and psychic energy, as Jesus pointed out when asked about the greatest commandment (Mk 12: 28 ff). This means that God is always the central point of reference when we his friends make decisions. The fall-out from this is that the friends of God—whose whole self is centered in Jesus–will also be open to love other people as friends, within the fullness of how Jesus does this. This is substantially different from the works of righteousness or mercy in scripture, for to do good for another, even to the point of dying for her, does not necessarily invite that person into your soul. Mercy does require some empathy, but not necessarily the eyes of Christ that bestow equality of dignity and intimate oneness and mutuality, which are intrinsic qualities of friendship. The friend sees opportunities to enhance the greatness of the other according to the dreams of God for that person, and works to enhance this greatness. Clearly, Jesus' idea of friendship goes far beyond the comradeship or intimacy of our usual interactions with friends. Someone once defined a friend as a person with "home valence," a person who is present within our psyche with all the power of *home*. In Jesus' mind, home was the Father, and it is into this mystery of affinity, of exchange of life, of roots, of union, that he invites all of us who love him.

A friend knows the other's minds and longings, sometimes even better than the person herself does. This was certainly the case with Jesus, whose insight into people's heart was total (Jn 2: 24-25). He knew the Father's heart and he knows ours. What he knows, then, is that, at deepest, our desire is to be at home with God, to be like him, to be united with him in love and to enjoy the fullness of life that comes from sheer loving and being loved. This means that, at our deepest, we long for single-heartedness. At the last supper Jesus reveals his own heart–his motives for doing the work the Father had given him–and makes them available to us by insisting that he is our friend and we are his. Friends are equals; friends have potential; friends are worthy and can respond to the gift of friendship that is extended. It is friendship that allows Christian chastity to flourish and grow into an extension of Jesus' friendship with every person. For this is Jesus' will: that we know the Father personally, intimately and lovingly. When this happens, God's love fills our world and his Kingdom comes on earth as is does "in heaven," that is, in the dynamic of love and life between the Son and the Father.

The second and third elements of friendship that Jesus mentions are that friends receive all that the Father gave Jesus and have full authority to put Jesus' person and work into play. What did Jesus receive from the Father? The Spirit, the work of making the Father known, the gift of being bread broken and eaten, of being light, of being the way, of doing the Father's work with God's own power and with full authority, of being good shepherd and servant, of being the personal place where the Father is worshiped in Spirit and in truth–and much more. Especially making it possible that we learn to be a friend to others, that we extend Jesus' friendship to others. So Jesus can say to us, his friends: "As the Father sent me, I send you" (Jn 20: 21). Or "If you forgive men's sins they are forgiven" (Jn 20: 23). Or "Cure the sick, raise the dead, cleanse the lepers, cast out demons" (Mt 10: 8). Jesus is our friend and whatever a friend has is shared. We are to become, be, what he is in every way. Thus Mark ends his gospel with the disciples going out, "while the Lord worked with them" (16: 20), that is, with our souls knit to his. In personally guaranteeing all that his friends undertake at his request, Jesus is giving us his own gift of single-hearted love. This means that there is objectively no limit to the power of Jesus' single-hearted friends to transform the world into the Father's Kingdom. The only limit is our subjectivity–our not keeping our relationship with him as our first priority. Mark says that when Jesus called his first apostles they were "to be with him, and to be sent out to proclaim the message, and to have authority to cast out demons" (3: 14-15). Of these three, we sometimes overlook the first, the being-with-him as friends, though it is the basis of everything else.

The greatest love, Jesus says, is to lay down one's life for one's friends (Jn 15:13), which he meant literally as he faced impending execution. He loved his own to the end, John says at the beginning of chapter 13. The friend of Jesus shares experientially in God's own steadfast love and extends it to others. As one of Shakespeare's sonnets has it: "Love is not love that alters when it alteration finds"–and Jesus' love, like the Father's, lasts to "the end." In God there is no chronological end, there is only life in a fullness that is always beginning, always in union and always complete. This is the invitation of Christian friendship: to be so united to Christ in friendship that every act of friendship we extend to others is his friendship extended; that every act of friendship extended to us by others shines for us with Jesus' friendship to us. Then we will be able to say with our last breath that the work is finished (as Jesus did on the cross) that, in a with him and as his friends, we not only looked after his sheep (Jn 21: 15 ff), but saw and served each one as a friend.

It is this kind of love that orients every other model of love– brotherhood, spousal love, even *agape*. It is the love at the heart of the Trinity.

REFLECTION GUIDE

Describe the two great friendships in your life. What was the relationship like? How did you care for one another? What would you change if you had it to do over again? How did the friendship end, if it did?

Of the four elements of friendship Jesus describes, which has functioned most centrally in your experience of friendship? Which have you experienced as joined to Jesus' relationship to you?

What have been the practical consequences of your working out of the metaphor of friendship with Jesus? What have been your greatest challenges is accepting and giving him your friendship?

14

Sister and Brother to Me

Then his mother and his brother came, and standing outside, they sent to him and called him. A crowd was sitting around him and they said to him, "Your mother and your brothers and sisters are outside asking for you." And he replied, "Who are my mother and my brothers?" And looking at those who sat around him, he said, "Here are my mother and my brothers. Whoever does the will of God is my brother and sister and mother." (Mk 3:31-35)

Jesus is our brother. A metaphor, and more than a metaphor, a doorway into the deepest message of the gospel–that we, in him, are God's beloved daughters and sons. For Jesus, the metaphor and the experience were one: he lived squarely in the mystery of his relationship to the Father. Raised from the dead, his first concern, as he sends Mary Magdalene off, was to unite us to his experience of the definitive love of the Father for human beings. Jesus gathers us into his own experience of being brother to us and open up this relationship to us, his sisters and brothers.

To find ourselves called into brotherhood with Jesus is at once the simplest and most difficult of the metaphors of single-hearted love. We all have our dream of the perfect family: truly loving parents who, focused on children's wellbeing, communicate to them everything that is good, true and conducive to happiness, and send them out to bring life to the world. And the children in such a family are all receptive, embracing their parents' path, lovers of God and others, and moving as adults into the wider world to enhance Christ's Kingdom. Brothers and sisters are mutually affectionate and helpful, and, as adults, become true friends to each other. Brothers and sister can count on each other in emergencies, rally together to support parents in old age, and help each other throughout their life. This is a highly idealized version of the human experience of the family as the basic unit of survival: we have to gain and share our resources and make common cause against enemies because we live in a hostile environment. Therefore, we love our brothers and hate our enemies, as we and the scribes sometimes interpreted scripture (Mt 5: 43-48). Some hardy idealists do try to live out of this model.

But the flesh-and-blood family is something else entirely. The parental role is theoretically the same, although parents play it out from within their own lack of integration. But the response of the children is different. Children are born into the family unformed, ready to be shaped. But, the ego discovered, the child itself determines the shaping. So parents can propose, discipline, counsel and pray all they want to, but by adolescence their moral power takes a back seat. Parents, however, are not the only molders. Some recent studies indicate that siblings have a powerful influence on the developing person. First of all, siblings spend more time interacting with each other than parents can spend. Secondly, siblings—even Christian ones—are not sources of parental goodwill. As we see in all the battles among siblings, they, too, are fallen: ego-driven, passion-driven, lacking in understanding of the world, lacking in compassion, lacking in any sense of what is best for the other as well as in desire to share the good they have. All such positive qualities must be learned within the family (and its extensions, the school and the church). We assimilate these qualities unevenly, and no one reaches adulthood a totally integrated and loving human being. The real family—as in the family saga in Genesis—is a chaos of murderous envy (Cain and Abel), greed and ambition (Jacob and Esau), jealousy (Joseph's brothers), injustice (the Ishmael/Isaac situation). Then, as now, the parents often generate the problems by preferring one child over another. The real family may be a conglomerate of very needy people competing for resources. Part of growing up is learning to compromise, share, think of the common good and, in a Christian family, give our resources away to someone who needs them more.

So our historical families are a mixed bag. Our brothers and sisters are the people who have shaped us into persons who know how to act in a world of equals. They are also the persons who have experienced most immediately the beginnings of our development–or lack of it–into a loving person. Our siblings, then, are the people who, for good or ill, have bumped up against us all along the way, teaching us how to bend and re-form; teaching us the consequences of our bad behavior by their anger, sadness and forgiveness; teaching us that the harm we do need not cut us off from their love, since there is always a tomorrow that will forgive, heal and move on. Like many animals, brothers and sisters recognize each other by smell, as it were. Having shaped each other, we are assimilated into one another's souls in very complex ways. Our brothers and sisters knew us before we put on the masks we have presented to the adult world. It is very difficult to deceive our siblings once they reach maturity, because we are the mirrors of each other's experience of learning to love God, ourselves, each other, the world. If there is not too much distortion and no one has been forced into a parental or subservient role, brothers and sisters may finally become friends, while allowing their lives to diverge and each to become his own person. There exists a *we* that cannot be denied except by violent rupture that will leave a yawning hole in our selves.

These remarks are only preliminary. Jesus asks of his followers that we "leave" father and mother, brothers and sisters, in order to follow him (Mt 19: 16-30), leave our human assumptions about relatedness behind. One consequence of this is that Christian love, flowing from oneness with Jesus, is primarily Father-centered. It flows directly from Jesus' own experience of his origin in God. The Christian is invited to move from a notion of God viewed objectively into an experience of God as Father–as the one from whose love we spring, in whose love we live and move and have our being (Acts 17: 28), and into whose love we are being transformed. Into an experience of God as an approachable, warm and helpful Dad. Into an experience of God willing to offer us up, his best-beloved sons and daughters, that the world might live (Jn 3: 17). The call into brotherhood with Jesus is a call into the kind of intimacy that allows us to be born into Trinitarian life and begin to develop into true sons and daughters of God, within a group of others who are also trying to give shape to their deepest identity. By forming ourselves into spiritual brotherhoods and sisterhoods (the Church and other associations), we lovers of Jesus are both claiming kinship with him and proclaiming to ourselves and the world that we are still on the way, that we are striving together for the kind of love into which sharing his sonship of God is calling us, the fullness of which none of us has achieved. But Jesus has and is thus our guarantee. The personal (rather than the political) history of the Church is a long sequence of such attempts, and have given birth to spiritualities in which this is the primary metaphor. Franciscans, for example, claim brotherhood as their central concern. The Charles de Foucauld communities have the same maxim: *Be brothers*. And, of course, St. Paul's communities.

Friends are friends because they are drawn to one another and forge the bonds of affection that lead them to lay down their lives for one another. Brothers and sisters are not chosen–they are simply there, a gift. It is with a deep sense of his followers as the Father's gift that Jesus makes his final prayer in John 17. And so the call into brotherhood is also a call into a vision of our self as a gift to Jesus and to the others; it is a gift for which it is worth laying down our life, a hidden treasure luckily discovered. If our faith were always single-hearted, we would open into this mystery with the joyous spontaneity of a St. Francis. Our real experience is that communities of brothers and sisters in the Spirit, whose egos are constantly knocking up against each other, are not always so single-hearted. Everyone knows that we generally bring into communities all the baggage of our families of origin, including not only unresolved conflicts with siblings and parents, but also our self-centered hopes and fears, anger and envy rising from the fact that our hearts are still divided, adulterous. Even Jesus had to face this problem, as we see in Mark 3:21, when his presumably well-intentioned brothers and sisters came, in a kind of intervention, to save him from what they considered a crazed lifestyle–by force if necessary. Being brothers and sisters is pervasively how the early Church perceived itself. The expectation that our communities will be made up of only single-hearted lovers of God and the sisters and brothers–Christians are idealists, after all–will be severely challenged by the incomplete single-heartedness of the real sisters and brothers. So what is to be done? First, we have to go beyond whatever limited models our society holds up to us. They are not apt to describe our brotherhood with Christ. Jesus says that we must "leave" our experiences of being sister and brother behind. Brotherhood with him lies solely in doing what the Father is asking of us. We are brothers and sisters because Christ has joined us to himself and is actively engaged in helping us know and do whatever he Father wills. This and this alone is the basis of Christian brotherhood, and it is the shape of single-hearted love of the Father and his plans for us in Christ. Christians gather into communities to help one another do this, and if they have a common work, to make sure the work is also Christ's work with reference to the Father. However in the experience of being brothers of the Lord, single-heartedness is family-like: each one of us, totally focused on God's will, is bumping up against all the others. Each of us knows we are not yet totally responsive to God's will and see that some of the dynamics of unredeemed ("fallen") family life do assert themselves, and so we can trip each other up.

Nevertheless, because Christ calls us into this relationship, he holds it together. We are also always bumping up against him, and his Spirit is life-giving. A close reading of the gospel stories before the resurrection show clearly that Jesus' single-heartedness was focused by his relationship with God as *Abba* (Father/Dad). Although he spoke widely of "my Father," he did not explicitly include his disciples in this experience. At most, he taught his followers to join together before God as "our" Father. But his death has bound us to him irrevocably, as his lifeblood has become the life of all those who love him–in fact, John's gospel has him giving birth to us on the cross, as it were. We would expect, therefore, that his first proclamation of his glory would be some kind of proclamation of our salvation or reconciliation or even mission. But no. What he is concerned about is the identity of relationship: our oneness with him means that he shares his relationship with the Father with us absolutely. Jesus saw his sonship in broad perspective. The Son comes from the Father (Jn 16:28), always hears his Father (Jn 8: 28-29), speaks what his Father speaks (Jn 7: 16), does his Father's work (Jn 10: 38), dwells in his Father's house (Jn 14: 2), is the Father made visible on earth (Jn 14: 9). The grace of the resurrection is to invite us into all this: Go to my brothers and sisters and say to them, "I am ascending to my Father and your Father, to my God and your God" (Jn 20:17).

The gospels present this relationship as something radical. In the epigraph to this chapter, Jesus deliberately shifts kinship with him from blood relationship to integrity of love for God: "Whoever does the will of God is my brother and sister." On Easter morning, Jesus gives Mary Magdalene the central mystery to be proclaimed: that together we are entering into Jesus' own relationship with God the Father. Entry into this mystery is so commonplace that many of us Christians simply take it for granted in our lives of response to God as Father, so commonplace that it may no longer seem metaphorical, becoming a plain fact so deep in our souls that it seems lacking layers of meaning. But for the rest of us this metaphor can come as a shock and the ever-opening up of a radical dimension of single-hearted love. It redefines who we are and makes it impossible to choose authentically anything lying outside God's will.

The placing of brotherhood within Jesus' sonship as the first proclamation of his resurrection needs to be taken seriously, not only as Jesus' proclamation of who he is, Son of the Father, but as the basic statement of who we are. It is only because his resurrection makes it possible for him to unite himself to us completely that we can claim our mutual sonship. Once we lay claim to it, we live out together–

Christ and each of us together—a single-hearted love with no other agenda, an almost transparent metaphor, as the simplicity of our union in the Trinity has no adequate parallel in human experience. Nevertheless we can recognize each other in the perfume of the Spirit. His primordial relationship will overflow into ours: we are brothers and sisters of Jesus because God has become our Father, *and* God is our Father because Jesus claims us as of one heart with him. We are his kin.

Sometimes, when we become discouraged by our own lack of perception and residual egotism, along with that of our fellow parishioners or community members, we may doubt whether brotherhood in Christ is anything more than a pipe dream. Sometimes, like the Jerusalem community in Acts, we are tempted to worry about who is letting in the riff-raff. It is in this kind of situation that we are called to allow God to make our hearts single, as he tells us that these, with all their limitations, are people whom he loves and whom he is giving us to love, just as he is giving them us, with all our limitations—and that our interactions will change us all, enrich us all. As the first letter of John puts it: "Those who do not love a brother or sister whom they have seen, cannot love God whom they have not seen" (4: 20, although the whole letter is apt). Brotherhood in Christ—as in the family—negotiates transitions. And brotherhood takes seriously all the Beatitudes, those of limitation as well as those of power. Particularly those of limitation, perhaps. For in the brotherhood of our real historical situation no one is fully integrated in love. God is at work in us all, with all our limitations—and his power, at work within our limitations, is made perfect in our weakness (2 Cor 12: 8). The task of chastity is to move us beyond our self-preoccupation and delusion of being so spiritual that we need no one, the illusion that the way to God is a great solitary, heroic quest. Then chastity makes us available to each other in our mutual need. On the day we can claim this experience of brotherhood in Jesus as an experience of a relationship with God as a Father, we become the new creation itself—Christ gives birth to me, to all of us. Then we begin to know what true brotherhood consists in.

It is only by dealing with real human beings that we discover how ambivalent our desire for God's will really is and how much we need the affirmation and support of one another in order to keep doing it. There are no supermen among Christ's brothers. But there must be a great tolerance for differences in interests, gifts and destiny. What Christ teaches his brothers is that one's giftedness does not demean another; rather it enriches all of us. St. Paul seems to have fully integrated this reality. First of all, he understood Christ's relationship to us as that of the firstborn among many brethren. The role of the firstborn, the heir, was to share out the patrimony so that all could live a full life. This means that Jesus stands among us, his brothers and sisters, as the radiating source of the Father's fullness, the glory of the Father's wisdom and love:

> *He is the image of the invisible God, the firstborn of all things hold together. He is the head of the body, the church; he is the beginning, the firstborn from the dead, so that he might come to have first place in everything. For in him all the fullness of God was pleased to dwell, and through him God was pleased to reconcile to himself all things...by making peace through the blood of his cross* (Col 1: 15-20).

To be Christ's brothers and sisters is to live toward this mystery. The second thing St. Paul says is that not only do we receive *from* Christ's fullness, but that we actually *receive* it, we become the fullness of Christ (see especially Eph 1). We are to be Christ's own single-hearted love. In Christ, we are to be radiant centers of God's will to love and serve the good of each other, without setting limits on what, how much or how long. We live within our human limitations, and no one can bestow all good on everyone. Even Jesus could not, until he was raised from the dead. But now he is present and active in and through us. If we accept his choice of us and remain united with him, he can and will gather more and more people into this great family that actively does the Father's will. Brotherhood is the spiritual path of those who know that they need to learn how to love concretely, practically, in small situations. Of all the expressions of single-hearted love, this is the one most willing to take life simply, to accept the gift of God's choice of companions and to share our life–Jesus' life–with them. As we look at the members of the real Church, not just bumping up against each other but sometimes grinding against one another like continental plates (we are so different and still unwhole), we begin to see that what is profoundly uncomfortable is the human way the Father's will is done: imperfectly by each of us, perfectly by all of us together, because Christ is our life and has the power to really accomplish much more than we can imagine, much less do.

When we find ourselves addressed as "brothers and sisters," then, we need to pause. This is an affirmation not just that we are brothers and sisters *of* Christ, but brothers and sisters *in* Christ. It is Christ's living of the Father's will that he communicates to us; thus we become in him sons and daughters of the Father, brothers and sisters to him. "Become" is the operative word. It will help us not to jump into sinful judgments about each other. Knowing that Jesus is working in us restrains us from attributing bad motives to behavior we do not like and keeps us from the suspicion that others will harm us if we do not defend ourselves against them. It keeps us aware that we are infinitely gifted and, though each has a different capacity to receive, all these gifts work for the good of all. But for those who know that we are all equal in God's love and need to help each other to love, and who approach every person with this kind of simplicity, love becomes single-hearted; the heart is wholed. We are all in this together single linewe "smell" alike, spreading the perfume of the knowledge of Christ everywhere, as St. Paul puts it (2 Cor 1: 14).

Recent books on Mother Teresa (especially that by Kolodiejchuk) highlight her absolute single-heartedness. She understood herself within a different metaphor, but from our perspective here we see in her what Jesus hopes for from his brothers and sisters: to do the Father's will only and always, moving out to one another in our need, as he did. And as did his mother, whose presence was the catalyst for Jesus' discovery of his brotherhood with us.

REFLECTION GUIDE

In your experience, what comes first: your sense of oneness with Jesus? your sense of oneness with the Father, which leads to you Jesus? or your sense of needing a spiritual group in order to discover Jesus? How has this shaped your growth in love?

What is the power of Christian brotherhood as you see it lived out in religious and secular groups around you?

Brotherly love is the love that is willing to admit to lack of body-spirit integration and help each other grow toward it. What is your experience of negotiating the transitions with the help of others also on the way?

For you, who is the saint who models the kind of brother or sister of Christ you would like be? What new ways of being and doing would this require of you?

15

The Community of the Beloved

In the gospel of John single-hearted love in all its dimensions focuses the meaning of Jesus' life and death. The thrust of all Jesus had done was to enter the hour of his glory, which came in his passion and was represented by the group of people gathered around Jesus at the foot of the cross. Jesus is the glory of the Father, the full, human manifestation of the Father's life-giving presence and action. Jesus is the beloved Son of the Father, the new and definitive Adam, the primordial Son of God. And he has come to reveal to us what it means to be fully human: to be able to love and lay down our lives for our friends. But Jesus is not alone on Calvary. He is joined there by his mother and his beloved disciple (to be understood in the plural, if we count the women). If Jesus is the archetypal man, his mother is there as the archetypal woman. So John is transporting us to the primordial garden: *Woman, here is your son… Beloved friend, here is your mother.* Man and woman creating a new race of people, forming the definitive community of love: Jesus, God's beloved Son; the disciple beloved by Jesus and the Father; and the woman who can mother the dynamic of loving. All of them loved single-heartedly by God. All of them loving God single-heartedly. A community of brothers and more than brothers. All of them bringing to birth the desire of God's heart in the simplicity of the Spirit's creating the new thing in water and blood. The single-hearted Church of love is born.

And this Church is a true community of the Spirit, because its heart is God's. Thus at the end, as at the beginning of creation, we see that single-hearted love is not something individualistic. Love binds together and creates something new. As married people may experience, this new thing is nothing less than the blaze of love between Father and Son made visible on earth. This is something that consecrated celibates have intuited and why they gathered into communities–even the hermits. The mystery of Trinitarian love has to be expressed, embodied. And this, beyond all that has already been said, is the reason for the Church. The community of the Church, like the community of marriage, expresses the dimension of God that no one can do as an individual: open a future in love, together.

As we have seen, Christian marriage can be appreciated only within the mystery of the friendship of each partner with Jesus and in an appropriate level of psycho-sexual development, discussed above. The communion of love requires that there be two distinct persons who choose to unite themselves by giving themselves in reciprocal love. Community expands from the communion of this *we*. There is the *we* of the couple and the family. There is the *we* of friendship. There is the *we* of mutual commitment to the good of the larger society. The impulse to merge into a *we* can be based in our biology (instinctive sexuality, eros); psychologically, in the vulnerability of our naked loneliness and need of friends; spiritually, in our soul's absolute need of God. To the extent that the *we* is forged, we find our life mutually enhanced: we are energized, happy, whole, together.

All three dimensions of human experience–eros, friendship, total self-giving–need to function in harmony, need to be integrated and lived within our relationship with God, or they will become distorted–biblically iniquitous. We humans have learned some profound things about human community in the hundreds of thousands of years we have existed. One is that the reproductive drive, though not an absolute value, is probably the strongest and most pleasurable we experience It is, however, irrational, and must be disciplined to the service of committed love, the creation of a *we* (as we observed in chapter 4). Another is that the search to become a *we* can take a variety of forms. It appears that, from Jesus' point of view, the normative community is that of friendship, not the procreating couple. In the debasement of our sexual mores today we can often see that neither forming a permanent *we* nor parenting is perceived as having major importance for the societal whole: we find ourselves in a pandemic of promiscuity, lack of commitment, divorce and rejection of children through contraception, abortion, abandonment and abuse. Sex often becomes a loveless, impersonal, self-absorbed pursuit of ecstatic pleasure.

Looking at our twenty-to-forty-year-olds who are not rushing into marriage, we do see the importance given to the dimension of friendship. What they seem to seek above all is intimacy, being able to share themselves as friends. However, unless a person discovers the next dimension, God's call into greater communion with himself, she will short-circuit her friendships by trying to make her friend or spouse provide her ultimate happiness or by trying to be the ultimate happiness of this friend or spouse. How many divorces happen because I find that I want more than my friend/spouse can humanly give me? Or I want to be the only person he cares about? Or I now want more than I did before? Or I feel stifled by my friend's possessiveness or indifference? Or I discover that what I thought was friendship (so-called friendship with benefits) was just a self-serving lie we mutually agreed to? Or I finally see that at its source the relationship has flowed from an adulterous heart, or from two? Many friendships eventually end–those that do not develop into single-hearted *agape*, commitment to live for the other in Christ, no strings attached.

But the friendship between God and us does not end, because it is based not in mutual attraction so as to overcome our existential loneliness (God is not lonely), but in God's desire to help us, his friends, be better, be more. Certainly, on God's part, there is unshakable commitment: I am here, I will never forsake you–the kind of love, which the bible calls *agape*. It is a love that constantly seeks to share one's goodness with the other, to give it to him freely, even if there is no corresponding response. It is a committed gift of the self. And committed means that it comes from such a profound place in the self that it can never be taken back, thus creating a future. Christian marriage presupposes this depth—a depth that is not often found in the average twenty-five to thirty-year-old walking down the aisle.

So what are we to conclude? That we are a sexually debased society doomed to loveless extinction? That modern people are incapable of committed love? That God's kind of love cannot exist in our world? That there is no one capable of Christian marriage today? That our young people (along with the middle-aged) are so developmentally delayed that these questions are not even being raised? That I, the author, am to take the word of a friend to whom I was explaining the concerns of this book: "I don't know anyone who would be interested in such a topic"?

Of course not. Because this is the kind of love Jesus has, and he is actively drawing us deeper into it.

This said, the call to single-hearted following of Jesus by married persons can be seen historically in the way Jesus sent out the seventy disciples—two by two. Thanks to centuries of clerical bias, we have failed to place this detail in the historical setting of how the good news of Jesus was actually spread—not just by extraordinary people like Paul, but by ordinary people like Priscilla and Aquila going about their business of making a living and concerning themselves with God's working in the world (See Acts 18). And by Roman soldiers spreading out through the empire, settling down and creating a new future. Two by two as often as not would be a married couple sent by Jesus into the ordinary situations of daily life: family, work, church.

In *Clowning in Rome,* Henri Nouwen said that "Married people, by their dedication to God in a life together, are signs of God's presence in this world." But what kind of presence are married people signs of? First and foremost, they are signs of the reciprocity of God's love. God is Trinity. In God, each person of the Trinity is constantly giving himself to the other and receiving the gift of the other in joy. The mystical writers speak of the kiss between the Father and the Son, who live together in a dynamic dance of love. Thus the married couple is a sign of the communion of God's love, the interaction of the kiss. In our individuality, we humans can feel very lonely; we are hard-wired to love and be loved, and so must reach beyond our individual self to the person who will be able to engage the loving and being loved, dynamically. When such a couple, called by Christ, enters into covenant with each other, married life begins to burn with God's own fire of love–and burns brighter and hotter the longer they love. The married kiss is a surrender of love to God within the surrender of love to each other. It creates single-heartedness and becomes the sacrament of God's single-hearted love for us. They are also a sign of the reciprocity of love God hopes for from all of us–a mutual commitment that holds nothing back, that gives of itself without calculating fifty-fifty or ninety-ten or ninety-nine-one. Married love is a sign of the absolute generosity of God with us. Thus it gives concrete shape to the ideal of all Christian communities.

In their relationship the married couple can integrate all the kinds of love: the search to discover the desirable beloved (eros), home valence (friendship), surrendering oneself for the other's good (*agape*), and the resultant communion (one heart, soul, mind). We have already noted some developmental dynamics of these loves, so do not need to repeat ourselves. The fire of God's love is not fully expressed by eros, which tends to move from center as other dimensions of love–friendship, self-giving and communion–grow in importance. But the fire of love can be an inexorable process, and sometimes we may tire of giving without always receiving what we need: we may begin to count the cost of loving. This is why marriage must be a covenant, a definitive whole-hearted, irrevocable giving oneself away, so to speak. Each spouse commits him- or herself, renewing this commitment, day by day in generous welcoming, tenderness and forgiveness, and, year by year, in grateful and joyful celebrations and renewal of the commitment to love. God's kind of love is an ongoing choice to give himself to the other, both within the Trinity itself and outwardly to us. Jesus' made this commitment to us whole-heartedly in life and death, and continues to do so in his glory. He is the guarantee that his friends will find this single-heartedness and the fullness of God's joy together.

Married love (all covenanted love, in fact) is the source of energy and creativity. As this energy overflows, the married couple reveals the Trinity not only present but also at work in all the details of daily life. We who are friends of Jesus carry his Spirit into our world. This means that what we do within the dynamic of mutual loving creates a way of approaching other people and serving them. It requires not just that we serve, but how we serve–in joy and spontaneity, in generous willingness, tenderness and forgiveness. Married love opens our eyes to see the beauty of what God is doing in real people. Married love teaches us how to befriend the people whom God places in our lives. Married love teaches us how to lay down our life for others in poverty and generosity. And married love finds joy in this single-hearted focus. Why? Because the married person strives to carry out and act out of all these forms of loving, day in and day out. If practice makes perfect, the married are the validation of all Jesus was saying at the last supper about laying down one's life–a transparent sign in the world of the mystery of Jesus' love to the end.

Marriage in Christ reveals the great surprise: that laying down one's life for the friend is not gloomy and deathful, as our divorce rate leads us to suspect. From his cross Jesus guarantees that it will be a joy and the fullness of life. True, marriages will be marked by episodes of selfishness, the small cruelties and betrayals that give rise to the humility and forgiveness that test and ultimately cement our willingness to love to the end. They will also be marked by losses and the separation that death of a spouse brings. But these things do not end love, as St. Paul affirms (1 Cor 13: 13), nor does death, as widows and widowers bear witness. Grief will give way to a greater singleness of heart, the singleness of heart based on the experience of being loved day in and day out, whether we deserve it or not. Lived day in and day out, married love finally becomes an experience of God's steadfast love for us. The death of the spouse then becomes a confirmation of the even-greater love of God in which we have lived but not always noticed. And it opens the door to a vision of God's great hope that nothing can prevent God's love entering the world ever more fully, not even death. It places itself at the service of this hope.

The unmarried share in this same dynamic. No individual can be a sign of the Trinity's love: she must live in the communion of laying down her life in love. Such single-hearted love is at the heart of each of the metaphors of union we are reflecting upon in this book. Single-heartedness will lead every follower of Christ to seek out her fellow travelers in the Spirit and form communities of the Spirit, a life together–sharing what the Spirit is doing among us and within each of us, as discussed in the previous chapter. This is the need that gathers celibates into convents, that gathers spiritual friends into all kinds of configurations (communities of two, three or twenty to live their faith together, in secular institutes, societies of common life, brotherhoods, sisterhoods, and be nourished for a wider service of the world). Unless we embody and speak to one another of this mystery of communion in God's overflowing love, we and our world will die of loneliness, not knowing the joy that God's love offers us. In *The Great Divorce*, C. S. Lewis describes hell as an exponential fleeing from each other. This is the dynamic of the world today, as we see the separation accelerating rapidly into a virtual everything, driving toward total isolation. In our electronic world people scarcely touch each other in a personal way any more, so we Christians need to offer the world salvation, true healing, in the form of the recovery of Christian community. Some of the newer communities understand this clearly. They gather in Christ to reflect together on how the Holy Spirit is leading them to explore new dimensions of God's sense of the world and to make themselves aware of the call that this represents. As they embrace new ways of bringing love into situations, they give dead and dying ways of acting a decent burial and move ahead, calling one another to respond ever more deeply in love.

The community at the foot of the cross is giving birth. What is being born is the Church as God sees us–a blaze of love, pristine (see Revelation 21-22). What we have done to this splendor–that radiant community that God is creating–over the centuries has not been able to obscure the mystery completely. We begin to see that in a great many ways–friendship, marriage, consecrated celibacy, life-giving service–the lovingness of God is lived out and is impacting our world. Not too visibly sometimes, if we look at the 2000 years of the Church's struggles, misdirection and general cussedness. Yet even at our worst, we have not been able to extinguish God's love—and God continues getting rid of the wrinkles and spots that mar the face of Christ's Spouse on earth. But God is not satisfied with cosmetics. This is eternal life—to know you and me whom you sent—Jesus said to the Father (Jn 17: 3). So where is this mystery made fully visible and desirable? As we have tried to see, its visibility, its glory, lies in our struggles for wholeness, for integration of body and spirit, for integration of the human with the divine for love, for the true communion of love—which is what is meant by Christian chastity.

The world is not yet fully a community of love, nor is the Church. We are all beloved by God, but not all have entered into the love of Jesus on the cross enough to love one another as he does. In general, we get side-tracked in our struggles to love because we look to the confused world for the true polestar. But when we look to Christ who is himself is our Way, he guarantees our arrival. Ultimately, his task and ours is the hungering and thirsting for righteousness that gives rise to single-hearted loving. There is no other way, but it is not a difficult way. It only seems so at the beginning because we start life confused and fragmented. Once we step out onto the path of love and are faithful to the journey, the mercy and gifts of God flood in upon us. We feel the struggle for singleness of heart, but also feel Jesus' power and gradually see the transformation he is making in us. We feel ourselves beloved. We see others beloved. We find God being loved even by the most wounded of us. And we surrender to the dynamic of single-hearted love in the community of love around Jesus who continues loving to the end. This is his glory and the meaning of his resurrection. And—for those of us who live in him—it is our hope.

REFLECTION GUIDE

What is the spiritual relation between communion of spirit and formation of community?

Why do you think John places the gathering of the Christian community at the foot of the cross? How has this metaphor played out in your life?

The purpose of Christian marriage is to create a community of love that is as generous and reciprocal as the community of the Trinity. In your experience where have you seen such a marriage actually incarnated? What were the qualities of single-hearted love that shaped this community?

In your opinion, is gathering into a small community of love as urgent an expression of single-heartedness as the writer asserts?

How does the thrust toward community show itself in your life?

16

Eunuchs for the Kingdom

"Whoever divorces his wife, except for unchastity, and marries another, commits adultery." His disciples said to him, "If such is the case of a man with his wife, it is better not to marry." But he said to them, "Not everyone can accept this teaching, but only those to whom it is given. For there are eunuchs who have been so from birth, and there are eunuchs who have been made eunuchs by others, and there are eunuchs who have made themselves eunuchs for the sake of the kingdom of heaven. Let anyone accept this who can." (Mt 19: 9-12)

    The duty of every good Jewish boy was to become a man by marrying and raising his children to be faithful to God's covenant with Israel. Some experts say that Jesus' choice of metaphor in the above teaching was a response to insults hurled at him for remaining unmarried. His failing to marry was suspect and had to be justified. And so we must conclude that his doing so was central to his relationship to God and people. In the above passage, by speaking hyperbolically of the castrated man, who according to the Law was to be shunned by the community (Dt 23: 1), Jesus reiterates the absolute priority of the Kingdom. The Reign of God is characterized by all the attitudes of heart we see in the Beatitudes, including, centrally, both hungering for righteousness and single-heartedness. So within all this, what is the point of being unmarried, celibate?

There are at least two ways we can understand what Jesus is proposing. The first is the obvious: a person may forego marriage for a greater good. The other hides within the metaphor itself: the person who does this will be permanently marginalized. Jesus could have used a less exaggerated metaphor than that of a eunuch, but since he does, he forces us into the realm of what many men fear most: loss of manhood, physically (castrated), psychologically (dysgendered somehow) and spiritually (cowardly and ineffectual). Not only that, but he does so radically. We must look carefully at Jesus challenge to this deep fear (which, making the necessary adaptations, applies also to women) of ultimate sterility.

Over and over, as God had in the Old Testament, Jesus met his disciples' panic over the inbreaking of God's presence in and around him, with the question, "Why are you afraid?" or with the reassurance, "Fear not." As suggested in the discussion of the Beatitudes, above, the center of Jesus' concern is that the Kingdom is here in Jesus himself: God is breaking in upon the world as sheer love. Radically, Jesus says. In its pristine form, Jesus says. In fullness, Jesus says. In my person, Jesus says. In the marriage of heaven and earth, Jesus says. In the fullness of life, Jesus says. In a great celebration, Jesus says. The kingdom is here, God is here. God-is-with-us: Emmanuel. I am here for you: Yahweh (LORD). So why do his followers draw back? Fear–the human reaction to an imminent evil–is an inappropriate response to the presence of the Kingdom. But we do fear, because, Jesus says, our faith is meager. Our hearts are absurd, not hearing clearly, deaf. We remain ambivalent, with heart divided. The single heart, however, is fearless (1 Jn 4: 18).

Jesus is calling us to look at who we are from a completely different perspective. If we knew God's love as Jesus did, if we constantly experienced his loving presence in us and in the situations of our life–if we were single-hearted–then our ambivalence would be healed. So Jesus is opening up the new possibility. Give yourself totally to me and to the Kingdom; spend all your energy for this relationship; opt out of the stereotypical roles that society wants to assign you, and look to me for new roles in a new world. The invitation to be a eunuch is roughly equivalent to the call to be a prophet, for both calls come from within a faith enlightened to a relationship with God that goes far beyond our limited human desire to make a living and raise a family, even though God's love lies at the heart of both Christian marriage and Christian work. Jesus' last exhortation, "Let anyone accept this who can," is very suggestive, for it is taking single-heartedness from the realm of an attitude toward God and his world, into the realm of choice, a deliberate covenant, a total commitment of one's life to the radical inbreaking of God. Doing so, it casts everything else in a secondary role. The call to this kind of prophetic commitment remains an invitation. It is not made radically to everyone, and even when offered, is subject to our freedom to choose. But when it is accepted, it binds a person to Jesus in the singleness of his mission.

This kind of covenant between God and human beings has always been embraced by some. Jesus himself, John the Baptist, Paul, some Old Testament prophets—and, of course, Jesus' mother. The virgins and widows that rose up in the earliest years of the Church. The ascetics—and after them the institution of monks and nuns, and, for two millennia, hundreds of thousands of men and women, consecrated to this mystery in all kinds of configurations. What kind of person would embrace so radical a covenant? First of all, those whose relationship with God allows them to see the absolute value of God and who hunger and thirst for righteousness solely within their relationship with the God who loves them. Why does Harry marry Sally? The dynamic is the same, except that, for the celibate person, God is the Beloved; even more, the sole Beloved.

As we observe people who once chose celibacy and later renounced it, we are forced to ask ourselves what went wrong. We ask the same question about divorcing couples. This is an issue that the whole Church wrestles with, as we see in the marriage tribunals which sweat over the competence of people to commit themselves irrevocably. Sometimes the answer is that the person lacked the freedom to commit himself and thus misread the call.

For those called to love by God's love, being celibate for the Kingdom is not a renunciation–it is a single-hearted choice of the first love, the unique Beloved beyond all other loves. It is a gift of the Spirit and thus an entry into the kind of relationship with God we see in Moses, the friend of God. Jesus' oneness with God is the definitive archetype, and Jesus is also our way in, by modeling, by invitation and by communion. Unfortunately, this mystical dimension has not always been clearly perceived–and substitutions have been made, considering it a safer or better way to God, or, in institutional form, a way of life that allows us to serve.

If consecrated celibacy so binds us to our heart's desire, why are Christians not flocking into this form of covenanted love? Developmental issues aside, since they are discussed elsewhere, I think that it is probably because we have not disciplined our desires or silenced our clamoring hearts enough to let ourselves feel the urgency of God's love. Many of us spend an hour a week trying to find God in the liturgy, but we are not always aware that God's love is animating and impelling us twenty-four-seven. Since we do not look for his love personally focused on ourselves, we do not experience it–though it is there, together with the call to surrender into it, if we choose. God is largely a God unknown, unperceived. Our relationship with God is often much more like the swings between forgetfulness of God and repentance that is the dynamic of the Old Testament, than it is like the whole-hearted response of Mary (Oh, let it be to me!), Elizabeth's articulation of the Spirit's movement in her (both in Luke 1). Or like the dynamic response of Jesus to his baptism and reception of the Spirit, and that of the disciples, who immediately left everything to follow him. Though one did turn back.

So to whom is Jesus addressing these words about being eunuchs for the Kingdom? Who can accept them? Intuition into the call to consecrated celibacy is the fruit of intimate prayer, of conversation with God that is the result of listening carefully to how he proclaims his love to us through all the channels of his choosing: scripture, tradition, historical events. From making the Spiritual Exercises, we know that such listening not only is possible, but also available to anyone who wants to hear, who hungers and thirsts to hear. As discussed above, the gifts of the Spirit are the permanent dispositions which make us docile in following the Holy Spirit's lead (*CCC*, 1830). These impulses of the Spirit assert themselves fully only when a virtuous life has freed us from destructive habits and when we have learned how actually to be a friend. "Docile" does not mean compliant, as in general usage, but rather, eager to learn. However, since the call to consecrated celibacy may come early in life, it may well precede the freedom to live it fully; it may be the merest embryo of the Holy Spirit that needs time and nurturing to come to maturity. But it is there. If we are to respond to the call of love, God must create a teachable heart in us. Our way of life can often be so frantic that we neglect the movements within–hence our need for the drama of mind-blowing awakenings and conversions. God tells the frightened and distracted citizens of Jerusalem: "In returning and rest you shall be saved; in quietness and in complete trust shall be your strength" (Is 30:15). It is a basic principle of the spiritual life that God cannot enter fully into the covenant of love he desires with us, unless we want to join with him. Therefore, our task is to ask for this desire–the insistent advice St. Ignatius gives in the Spiritual Exercises– to imagine God constantly at the door of our consciousness and to open ourselves to his choice of us in love.

Once we embrace the covenant in the form of giving ourselves completely and exclusively over to God's action in us, the shadow emerges: permanent marginalization. It is difficult enough for a Christian trying to live a chaste life, to fit into an eroticized society. Today plenty of people are willing to remain unmarried if they can pursue their sexual urges ("fulfillment") without interference. But singleness without sexual pleasure–much less true chastity or celibacy for the Kingdom–is unintelligible to them. This has its parallel in marriage. Plenty of married people have substituted sex for love within their marriages and extramaritally, so a clear call to grow into a love that leads them deeper into the God of love at the heart of their marriage is equally unintelligible. The Christian commitment to God's kind of love guarantees minority status. Like the prophet, the eunuch stands at the city gate, a puzzle and a reproach. The puzzlement is obvious–our society has no convenient stereotypes by which to evaluate such an oddball. The reproach lies, I think, in the fact that a lifestyle different from the accepted norm can actually be chosen and maintained, as we saw in Augustine's story. The reproach is concretely present and ongoing. Eros in this country is not really intentional; we are manipulated like the famous Gerasene swine–and like them, are drowning. As an unreflective society, we are slaves to our drives, so that a person freely celibate for the sake of the relationship with God is an implicit criticism and an irritant. The person joyful in the loving service of others is a danger, since she forces us to reflect. Some degree of alienation from what everyone thinks and what everyone is doing is inevitable. The consecrated celibate lives out prophetic homelessness, and loneliness can be a consequence. The person called by God to celibacy has no option except her growing intimacy with God and her loving the world as God does.

The permanence of the covenant of consecrated celibacy also contains a shadow (as does the permanence of marriage). Once I have freely given myself to him, I am God's: God is free to do with me as he wishes. Because I have given my self away, there is no way I can take back the gift, no way I can undo what I have done. No annulment is possible (unless there was some serious lack of freedom, already noted above). The good news is that God will honor this gift of self in the development of deeper friendship or of a spousal relationship or the relationship implied in the other metaphors we are discussing. Even better news is that it provides the structural stability for the development of the mystical life, including all the difficult times of purification and transition. For the chosen person there is no alternative to growth in love, the Kingdom on earth. No alternative to a growing hunger and thirst for righteousness, except loss of his soul, his self. It is a communion in Jesus' true priorities. By calling the person into this kind of relationship, he guarantees its accomplishment. But what a level of faith it demands of the person called! No wonder the prophets tried to squirm out of their call. No wonder we sometimes do!

The single-hearted eunuch is God's comment on the American eleventh commandment: *Thou shalt seek life, liberty and the pursuit of sexual fulfillment.* A life given away free may be perceived as un-American. It is ironic, then, that the person who has relinquished her very self will certainly have to defend this self against spoken and unspoken criticism:

> *Let us lie in wait for the righteous man,*
> *because he is obnoxious to us*
> *and opposes our actions;*
> *reproaches us for sins against the law…*
> *He became to us a reproof of our thoughts;*
> *the very sight of him is a burden to us,*
> *because his manner of life is unlike that of others…*
> (Wisdom 2: 12-15)

Such alienation in matters great or small can be crucifying. God's comment in Genesis that it is not good for human beings to be alone is particularly important in a modern climate of incomprehension. The consecrated celibate needs to love and be loved in non-erotic ways. And so the person called must find others called to walk the same path, a community of brothers and friends, as we see in chapters 13-15.

Eunuchs, natural and man-made

Consecrated celibacy—the response to the call to belong exclusively to God the Beloved—is a gift God offers and it is accepted by those who can and want to respond to such love in kind. But what about those who find themselves unmarriageable because of laws, custom or trauma? When God observed that it was not good for a human being to be alone, he was understating the problem. A loner scarcely develops as a human being; he is a danger to himself and others. Pope John Paul II speaks of our primordial state as being what he calls "original solitude," but in real life the best we can do is to hope that we will get to solidarity by way of singleness of heart. Today we see at least four situations of those suffering a singleness imposed on them from without: the divorced, homosexuals, the abused and those living on the threshold.

The divorced

It does not go well with loners, says God. Then Jesus comes out strongly against divorce and remarriage. There are two versions of Jesus' teaching on divorce in Matthew 19:

> *(1) Whoever divorces his wife, except for unchastity, causes her to commit adultery, and whoever marries a divorced woman commits adultery.*
> *(2) Whoever divorces his wife, except for unchastity, and marries another, commits adultery.*

True, once one has intentionally and freely given oneself away to a spouse in love, there is no ethical way one can take back the gift. But divorce does happen and did happen in New Testament times. In Jesus' day, what would happen to a divorced woman? She would be cast out of her husband's clan, losing her children in the process. Then, without resources, how would she support herself? The story of Naomi and Ruth illustrates the problem. The only social ntework for a women without husbands was that their sons would inherit their share of tribal land and support their mother—if there were sons and if they had not lost their land. When the system broke down, the clan would rally round the widow, as did Boaz, to keep the land in the family.

But the divorcée was permanently marginalized unless she remarried. In fact, she had to remarry if she were not to be beggared or become a permanent burden on her family of origin. Jesus seems to be saying that the man who married her, no matter how well intentioned, would be complicit in the adultery. But what adultery? Hers? No, because she did not divorce her husband. He divorced her, as Jesus observes, to marry someone else. The only "adulterer" so far is the divorcing husband. So Jesus seems to be saying that the problem in marrying a divorced woman is that it makes the second husband complicit in the adultery of the first. In other words, Jesus is talking about a whole social system that places women and children–the family itself–at the whim of a refusal of love and commitment that can allow one to walk away from the person one promised, swore, vowed to care about. Today, in our society, women have more economic options and may be initiating the divorce. But in most of the world they still do not–and this is the context out of which Jesus is speaking. Speaking to us today, he would be gender-inclusive.

So then, what is Jesus saying? Not what the disciples immediately conclude–that no one wants to commit herself irrevocably to love another, so staying single is better. Rather that, amidst the breakdown of commitment, one should see the situation of aloneness as an opening into a new dimension of single-hearted relationship with God. With a 50% divorce rate among Christians today, Jesus is offering a radically new beginning to a great many people, the gift of celibacy for the Kingdom. What he is saying to heterosexual married persons applies also to homosexual persons in committed relationships. The Christian is in no way to become complicit in an ethic that permits rejection and abandonment of a person to whom one bound oneself to love. There are wedding customs in which the couple is roped together. As Genesis puts it, they are no longer two but one flesh. And "flesh" implies, beyond sexual union or children, mutual loyalty. The ultimate sin is disloyalty, lack of commitment, failure of steadfastness–these failures against the ultimate qualities of God's love.

These comments should not be construed as advocating homosexual marriage or as a condemnation of injured parties who are economically or psychologically incapable of going it alone. But they are an invitation to honor our commitments at a depth unsuspected when we first made them. Stay with your partner and learn to love him as God does. Failing this in divorce, the rejected person–in her single-heartedness–is being called to embrace her undesired singleness for the sake of a deeper, more radical commitment to God, who now offers himself to her as the unique Beloved. The person can choose to be a eunuch for the Kingdom. This is a new road of faith, an invitation to the divorced person to explore new dimensions of the Kingdom: from the Beatitudes of limitation into those of empowerment via single-hearted love. All it requires is that the person open herself to the presence of God's love in her situation.

Homosexuals

What is possible to the divorced is also possible to the homosexual person. In a special way, this exclusive relationship with God is offered to the Christian homosexual, who is particularly marginalized by societal prejudices. Add to this that the gay subculture is eroticized in promiscuous adolescent forms and that structures of communities of non-eroticized love are apparently rare. So the first step the homosexual Christian must take is to step out of the gay mainstream and begin to look for companions who are capable of real friendship. This demands detachment, great singleness of heart, and moving toward expressions of love that are not eroticized. This is urgently necessary because there are few models of single-hearted love among gay adults. Heterosexuals have it easier in that by age twenty-five or so society starts expecting that they seek to marry and take on a responsible social role. But not all homosexual groups do this, and societal prejudices and laws may make doing so extremely difficult. So speaking practically, where can calls into friendship in self-giving love be realized? Historically, religious communities and societies of common life, structured on brotherhood and friendship, were a life-giving option, as they still are. Today there are also secular institutes and small Christian communities that can support the friendship and intimacy needed for the deepening of love. The homosexual has options which permit love to grow as committed friendship and brotherhood without eroticizing it. As with the divorced person, the Christian homosexual who is deepening his response to God is also in a liminal situation: God is opening the way of life-giving Christian celibacy, and he can move beyond a sense of victimization or self-hatred, choosing God the Beloved freely and joyfully, without the swamp of recrimination that often catches hold of and swallows up the divorced person.

The abused

There are also all the people who, because of early emotional or sexual abuse, have been paralyzed in their ability to trust others. They have learned to defend themselves against sexually-expressed abuse, often by repressing the sexual dimension of personhood. A long-range effect of this is often violent self-hatred. Such people need therapy. Along with therapy, spiritual direction can help them recover or discover trust in God that opens them to a relationship of single-hearted love for God. Multi-level healing is possible. Enabling a person to trust and love others and God is the great privilege of the Christian therapist, who becomes the model of the friend. Then, with substantial healing and the awakening of the human capacity for friendship, Christ's invitation into celibate consecration to him may be extended and embraced, even by people who may never be whole enough to be able to enter into a true marriage.

Those on the threshold

Finally, there are the ever-hopeful, who desire the companionship of marriage but have reached mid-life without finding their soul mate. Though lonely, many seem not to perceive that there are alternate forms of commitment to love. The shared commitment of married life is the only metaphor that calls to them: chosen celibacy has not revealed itself as their path. And so they seem always to dangle in hope of something unrealizable. As there are many people in this situation today, we need to ask why this is so. Is it that God simply will not overcome the societal forces at work–a historical impasse–or does this represent a spirituality of our age: people living powerless to command the completion of marriage? Spiritually speaking, feeling incomplete is not bad, as it will lead us to let go of our delusion that God is not enough. A sense of incompletion can bring the unmarried person to rest in his autonomy and can lead him to open himself to the other kinds of love, moving from loneliness to solitude, as Henri Nouwen insists we must. In a society that insists that happiness lies only in marriage while simultaneously resisting the commitment of marriage, the person who binds himself to God alone can become a sign of hope and of a full life rooted in a life beyond coupling. It may not be the form the person prefers or desires, but it can be a spiritual path with all the ascetical rigors we see in the desert hermits of antiquity. Although many a call has come at mid-life (e.g., Teresa of Avila, Ignatius Loyola, Augustine), those on the threshold, who are not conscious of a call to see their situation from a different perspective, remain in limbo, neither eunuchs for the Kingdom, nor not. For in Jesus' mind, celibacy is a matter of conscious and free choices. For such people, one of the other metaphors must function or love will remain incomplete.

With all these groups who are living the Beatitudes of limitation, what is the tipping point? Will they become embittered, angry people or will they inherit the Kingdom? The answer lies in their hearts. Can they tell God: I'm all yours, do with me as you like? The single heart is surrendered. From this surrender, Jesus insists, the fullness of life will flow.

REFLECTION GUIDE

Embracing the Kingdom celibately and single-heartedly requires that we overcome fear. As you look at your own areas of ambivalence, what seems to be the root of fear?

What spiritual steps do you need to take to make the Kingdom an absolute priority in your life?

"Being celibate for the kingdom is not a renunciation—it is a single-hearted choice of the first love, the unique Beloved beyond all other loves." What kind of spiritual experience does this entail? What would the development of celibacy look like in the young person and in the mid-lifer?

Among those who are unmarriageable for historical reasons, which group is most in need of pastoral attention? If you are in one of these groups, reflect on your specific pastoral needs. How might you reach out pastorally to people in these groups?

17

Bride of Christ

Men and women differ, but since everyone has both a masculine and feminine approach to things, this statement is not asserting that men act one way and women another. Nonetheless, men and women do take distinct approaches, masculine and feminine, to the mystery of Christ and his Church, and certainly to celibacy for the Kingdom. The poetry of mysticism often speaks in marriage metaphors: the soul, the Church as bride of Christ. Sometimes American Christians, both women and men, gagging on nineteenth-century religious sentimentality, have trouble with what they perceive as gender stereotyping. So they cannot relate to this metaphor at all or speak only reluctantly of being bride of Christ. Nonetheless, as the spiritual life develops, the intimacy and oneness between the risen Lord and his beloved become clearer, most are able to integrate this metaphor by moving beyond it, into experience: I have been chosen by Christ and choose him to make our future together. There is an additional reality that opens up to those men (and women) specially called to care for others: the role of spouse of the Church. The leader (pastor, shepherd, minister) embodies Christ's love for the Church, in the Church, and hence embodies also Christ's spousal commitment. For the sake of clarity, we will discuss these two realities separately, here and in the next chapter. Since the focus here will be on the Church as bride, I will use a primarily feminine vocabulary–without intending thereby to exclude men.

First, we need to understand the experience of being a spouse of Christ. For the sake of simplicity, we will focus on three dimensions: bride, consort, mother. These three are not necessarily successive; they cohere in each other and manifest themselves according to circumstances. One more note before proceeding. It is generally assumed that only celibates enter into this relationship with Christ. Not necessarily. As the spiritual experience is multi-dimensional, a married woman may find that her marital relationship a sign and entry into the deeper reality of her relationship with God in Christ–which is why marriage is considered a sacrament. It is important not to reduce any of these metaphors into something less than spiritual and then impose cultural stereotypes on them. It is simply that, up till now, the celibates have written the books.

The bride of Christ has gotten all the attention in the literature on consecrated celibacy, probably because this grace is so often filtered through a reading of the marriage poems in the Song of Solomon. What we have sometimes failed to take into consideration is the shift in perspective that happens when people at different stages of body-spirit integration (see Part II) are called into such a relationship. For hundreds of years, the working model has been the young woman in search of her mate. After all, the convents were constantly repopulated by girls, so the rituals surrounding their embracing their call to single-hearted love were bridal: rings, veils, bridesmaids. Different cultures and different times weighted all such symbols differently, but the psychology was clearly that consecrated celibacy is a marriage to Christ. Even a liturgy as solemn as the rite of consecration of virgins calls upon Christ to be a good husband: to cherish, comfort and support the bride in her new life, which, because it was a life in the Spirit, would involve spiritual growth and the way of the cross. All of this served to focus psycho-sexual energy toward the commitment that formed the bonds of loving communion that would impel the young woman's life into the future.

A wedding is exciting and deeply significant, but the task of newlyweds is to discover whom they have actually married and reconfigure their love to this reality as it is newly discovered, day by day. It is not precisely Jesus the human being who calls and consecrates the person, but Jesus, the risen Lord, the Word of God, divine Son of the Father. So discovering who this divine Other is, becomes the crucial task of single-heartedness, as the Song of Solomon indicates. The myth of Eros and Psyche is another way of understanding this dynamic. Eros (the god of sexual love) comes by night and Psyche (the soul) is forbidden to look at him: her happiness lies in preserving and entering more deeply into the mystery. The inevitable happens, of course. Knowledge, awakened, destroys the paradisal dream state, Cupid/Eros flees, and union has to be regained by a long search and hard work.

However, in Christian spiritual experience, knowledge is not only not forbidden but it is absolutely essential for single-hearted love. Our God is a God who reveals himself, who wants to be known and loved as he truly is, and who became human so that we might know him intimately. There is an old theological saying: *Acta Dei, verba Dei*–God's actions are his words. It is God's revealing Word that becomes incarnate in Jesus. So the first prerequisite to being Bride is to meet Jesus as the Word being spoken by the Father. And not only to meet him, but to allow this Word to totally transform her heart (mind, sensibility, decision). This is the logic behind periods of novitiate, seeking answers to the ultimate questions: Are you looking for God in Christ? Do you want to commit yourself to a single-hearted relationship with God exclusively? Are you ready to constantly explore the heart and dreams of God for yourself and for the world around you? Are you willing to join Christ as he engages God's heart and puts the dreams in play? So the bride is impelled into God's vision, into God's imagination, into his creativity.

The first task of the bride, then, is contemplation–always finding the Beloved at work in everything. Frankly, this is the work of a lifetime; but it begins from the first moment of the call and sustains the rest of the spiritual journey and the work necessary for its progress. Married couples whose relationship is drying up are always counseled to reestablish communication, and there are retreats, workshops, counselors available to help them. To love God, celibates have to know him, say theologians, for the will is blind: the heart has to reveal him as absolutely loveable. Single-heartedness lies in this "absolutely." The last episode of John's gospel is the account of Jesus appearing at lakeshore, unrecognized by the fishermen until the beloved–the disciple Jesus loved–cried out. Love sees. The Bride is first and foremost the one who recognizes her Beloved wherever he is, and only secondarily, the one who hauls in the nets. This seeing is the quality generally attributed to the contemplative nun, although restricting the call to a retired life is a stereotype, as we see in the lives of actively engaged mystics like Catherine of Siena, Teresa of Avila, John of the Cross, Padre Pio. But it is the heart of the call to everyone who chooses Jesus as the unique Beloved.

Once the bride has surrendered herself to Christ, there will be plenty of net-hauling. And in the course of working jointly with him, the bride becomes a consort, a true partner. Brides are one thing, wives are another. Look at marriages beyond the honeymoon: wives work, wives raise children, wives help plan for the future, wives call their husbands to move deeper into their souls, and on and on. Wives are not sweet, pampered darlings to be infantilized, coddled and patronized, no matter how much some women and men would like this to be so. That same story on the lakeshore has Jesus asking his friend Peter if he loves him enough to lay down his life for him (*agape*), and when Peter gives a threefold yes, Jesus entrusts him with his beloved Church. Psychologists talk a great deal about empowerment, helping people reach their potential. The spouse of Christ is called to move beyond her limited potential into the infinite power of Christ. Since Christ's task is nothing less than the fullness of life for everyone, there is no way anyone sane could presume to do this. But spouses are not two separate people living under one roof. Spouses are joined, heart, soul and spirit: they are friends united in intention and strategy and they place all their gifts at the service of the other. They work together. In the case of the spouse of Christ,

Jesus does most of the work, since he is able to give his life and Spirit directly to his beloved and to others through her. This is why the spouse can do the seemingly impossible. Women's enormous capacity for love makes them astonishing workers in the long haul. Working in union with Christ is what turns the bride into consort, equal to Jesus in dignity and with full access to his power. Otherwise, how could one ever explain the Mother Teresas of the world?

These two functions of the spouse of the Word–bride and consort–have formed the basis of the Christian understanding of Mary. Unfortunately, artistic and theological representations of Mary have often placed saccharine emphasis on some unworldly virgin lost in God–the sweet, pampered darling already adverted to. But this is unworthy of the Mary of the gospels and Christian experience. As spouse of the Word, she took the Word to heart, in the richest sense. As consort, she jump-started Jesus' mission in Cana, and has been active in the history of the world ever since. Scratch the surface of any Catholic or Orthodox Christian and you will find at least one story of how Mary has intervened in her life. Mary is the archetype of the Church as bride of Christ, and is the model for and mentor of each and every Christian, especially of those whom Christ calls into this relationship exclusively, the consecrated celibates.

The third dimension of the spousal relation with Christ is mothering. Over the centuries theologians reiterated that Mary's motherhood of Jesus is the basis of all her other gifts of grace. But she was mother only by virtue of her faith and her willingness to engage the Kingdom single-heartedly, as we see in the Annunciation story. Her motherhood of Jesus was a great gift, but from the cross Jesus gives her a greater gift: motherhood of all the sons of God. Her task–united with that of Jesus–is to nurture and make grow the life that flows from Jesus as he pours himself out in love for the Father and for his beloved friends. And this is the task she extends to all Christ's brides. Watching mothers age brings an understanding of how expansive motherhood is. At first it is simple: feeding and clothing the children, protecting them, expanding their world by exposing them to the best thinkers, artists, entertainers and lovers of God.

Then it becomes counseling, counseling, counseling–long after they have left home. Then worrying about, praying for, letting them take full responsibility for themselves. And after, this the grandchildren. Whatever brings fuller life and joy is the province of the mother. Mothers do not wait to be asked–they see, they love, they intervene. So Mary also becomes the model for this function of the spouse of Christ. He says to each of his consorts: "Here is your son," or "Feed my sheep." And he knows that the spouse will find creative ways to bring God's sons and daughters into union with him. Womb to tomb.

This third dimension is really a specification of being consort, but it is the dimension that others feel most directly and hence impacts others as an experience of God's mercy in their lives. And it is why the faith could survive during times when people were most alienated from the false god which the theologies of the day proposed to them. As we see in Mary's interventions, the spouse of Christ incarnates Christ's love. At the end of his life Jesus insisted that if we see him, we see the Father. The spouse of Christ says the same: If you see me, you see Jesus with me, and if you see couple love, you see the Father mothering, the Trinity itself.

REFLECTION GUIDE

The bridal metaphor focuses on the experience of discovery that one is loved single-heartedly by God himself. What dimensions of this discovery have you personally experienced?

How has your desire to know Christ more directly and intimately grown over the years? What awakened it? What steps did you take to embrace it?

The consort is fundamentally in union with Christ in everything and exercises his power. Who are the people who embody this metaphor for you? What were their main struggles along this line? Does this metaphor clarify your idea of your own role in the exercise of Christ's power?

To what extent does your idea of Mary cast her into the role of "sweet pampered darling" or that of one who can jump-start Jesus' mission?

Mothering constantly takes the form of helping people grow up. Who have been the spiritual mothers in your life? How have you experienced God's mothering in your concern for others?

18

Bridegroom of the Church

Let this mind be in you that was in Christ Jesus
Phil 2: 5

In scripture, "heart" signifies a dynamic interplay of mind, soul, desire and decision. In singling out the metaphor of Christ as Bridegroom as a model of single-hearted love, we enter into the mystery of God's free choice of us; of God's joining his life to us; of God's opening a new future with us; and of God's giving life to the world through us. Jesus is the catalyst for all this. John the Baptist first articulated this mystery when he insisted that his role was simply that of the "friend" of the Bridegroom–the best man, as it were. The only time Jesus used the image was in the context of the inappropriateness of fasting as long as the bridegroom is present (Lk 5: 34). Paul develops the ideas in Ephesians 5: 22-30: Christ loved the Church and gave himself for her. But it is the Johannine community that honed in on the ideas–the new Adam and new Eve on Calvary, and the marriage of the Lamb at the end of the book of Revelation.

But what does it mean for a person (man or woman) to be called to join Christ in the mystery of his espousing the Church? What are the implications of being called into the mystery of laying down one's life to the end, the mystery of the cross? First of all, such a call joins a person to Jesus as prophet and servant, functions that were coupled from Old Testament times, as in the Servant Songs in Isaiah 40-55. The prophets are also friends of God, as Jesus notes at the last supper, where he shifts us from the relationship of servant to that of friend (see Ch. 13, above, and John 15: 15). In doing this he makes clear that this friendship is prophetic–we know Christ's mind and his heart and we are sent out to help others also know them.

The bridegroom empties himself of all self-seeking and joins himself to the bride, so that the bride may live fully in God's self-giving love. The call to join with Jesus in the service of God's beloved people is to become a transparent presence of God's saving mercy. For example, in Philippians Paul, describes Jesus' service as total emptying of self in obedience, that is, on the model of the Father himself. Mark's gospel, in its no-nonsense describing of Jesus in action, is very suggestive: Jesus engaged people, singly and in groups, and let God's healing power simply flow through him. Mark describes Jesus' actions, not on his reflection on them–a kind of living out of Jesus' conviction that they are happy who hear the word of God and do it.

Jesus calls us to join with him in being his mercy in the world. What can we expect to happen? First of all, we discover that moving into oneness with Jesus, into his single-hearted love, is the work of a lifetime. Along with this, we soon learn that this single-heartedness has to have matured beyond religious ideology with its accompanying quackery, into real integrity and communion. The call may come to the spiritual beginner, but fruitfulness depends on maturity in the Spirit. Secondly, such oneness demands that our minds and hearts be soaked in Jesus' Spirit, that we know him intimately and love him deeply–that we live a life of prayer. Third, oneness demands that we see the situation of the real people around us with Jesus' eyes and that, like him, move into the deepest concerns of God for each person whom we encounter. Fourth, oneness demands that we discern not only what God desires for the fullness of life of each person, but what practical steps he wants us to take and in what spirit he wants us to take them. When Jesus calls us, he offers us a way to such prudence and wisdom. So the fifth expectation is that we will acquire these virtues the only way that they can be acquired–by continuing to love amidst the slings and arrows of life that are our share of Christ's suffering for the Church. Or, more succinctly, we will learn the wisdom of the cross.

This mystery of pouring oneself out, even to the point of death, so that others may live God's love, is what Church ministry is all about. Often, when we find ourselves called into a lifetime of service, we unconsciously carry our American preconceptions with us, especially the expectation of success. We want to pour ourselves out, but, like Jesus, find that people do not necessarily want God's Spirit in their lives. This should not be too surprising, since we have all experienced resistance to God's action in our own lives; however it sometimes comes as a shock, and we are stymied by frustration and self-doubts. Or we are tempted to become disillusioned and bitter.

The bridegroom of the Church cannot be a dreamer: the real Church is a bride full of spots and wrinkles. Yes, there are the committed single-hearted seekers who follow Christ in love and take up his mission energetically. These will understand and value our call and service, although they may not always agree with us about how to proceed (Paul and Barnabas in Acts of the Apostles come to mind). Then there are all the others. There are fundamentally unevangelized people on the fringes, cultural Christians, whose roots are shallow and who may be highly resistant to the discomfort of growth. These are the people who do not show up with any regularity, but who will rise up in vocal revolt when the good news contravenes their comfortable preconceptions. There are also the people in full revolt against God's action, the closet atheists in the Church, whose spirit is shackled by American cultural values and who can be vicious in their attack on spiritual realities they have never experienced and hence do not understand. These are the people who, in Jesus' words on the cross, "do not know what they are doing." There are also the spiritually unawakened, people of basic good will who are sidetracked into comfortable causes and devotions that are merely peripheral to the gospel and who settle happily for crumbs—Hobbit Christians, as it were, capable of love but too long unchallenged. There are also the inarticulate souls who long for God unreflectively and who intuit a connection between the minister and Christ, respectfully put him on a pedestal, but remain childishly passive and immobile, unaware of the urgency of interiorizing the Kingdom. The challenge to the person called to be bridegroom with Christ is to bring all these people into single-hearted love.

As this is obviously a humanly impossible task, the cross will come in a wide variety of forms. And it will come indeed, if only because, no matter how we may try, we cannot be "all things to all men," as Paul tried to be and failed.

We want to give ourselves, and, as we become more and more single-hearted, we truly become more transparent to Jesus' action in the world. We may, like Jesus, truly empty ourselves. This is a goal of single-hearted love. However when the self-emptying and self-gift are real, our situation can become very uncomfortable, for then we may simply disappear. People will often take us for granted–with the shrug that makes sure we know clearly that it is our job, our place, to serve. This is sometimes the approach of the Church's materialistic faction. Most commonly in the Church, it means that we will be considered mere service providers or human resources. People may fail to perceive the personal interaction that Jesus initiated and maintained with his disciples and with others like the Samaritan woman (Jn 4) or the Syrophoenician woman (Mk 7). This failure of perception is what Jesus complained about to the crowd: that they were following him, not because they saw in him the way into the Father's love, but because they were getting fed (John 6). The upshot of this was that he lost most of his disciples.

Being invisible often can create tension. Is selfless loving supposed to make us doormats? Are we called for the community only to be eaten alive? Jesus was not, nor are we. Like him, we are called to give life, to call others into single-hearted love. Consequently not every demand people make will actually help them find the Kingdom. And some situations may be irremediable: invincible ignorance or terminal hard-heartedness in people at large or in ecclesiastical superiors. Not every bishop or pastor is of Jesus' mind. To find ourselves in such a quandary, then, should not depress us.

It was the way that Jesus had to go, and it killed him. The grain of wheat that dies, he said, will bear a hundredfold. And it has, in him and in all those whom he has called along this way.

The Last Supper narrative in John's gospel begins: "Having loved his own who were in the world, he loved them to the end" (Jn 13: 1). Single-hearted love of Christ the Bridegroom means joining him on the cross of being sheer mercy for others. Happy are the merciful, Jesus said—and he knew that mercy always finds concrete expression (see Chapter 2, above). Bearing God's mercy may a blessing unperceived by the world, as Randy Newman famously sings in "Fool in Love": *Show me a man who is gentle and kind, and I'll show you a loser.* But the mercy that calls each person into single-hearted love of God is treasured by the Church made Bride, which lives consciously within the mystery.

When individual Christians fail to notice or appreciate the gifts the bridegroom brings, the minister then finds himself in the situation of Catherine of Siena. God told her: "I have placed you in the midst of your fellows that you may do for them what you cannot do for me: love them without receiving any return." In the end, the minister lets go of any residual calculation and is left with the naked mystery itself: Christ's call to be his love, with the intimacy and communion this call includes. To be his love and to love, as Jesus did, with a heart full of hope in what his Spirit can and will accomplish.

REFLECTION GUIDE

What differences do you see between being the bride/consort of Christ and being bridegroom of the Church? How are these metaphors alike?

What dimensions of spiritual integration would you expect to find in those whose commitment to Christ takes the form of laying down their lives for the Church?

Give examples of good shepherds you have encountered in the Church. How did these ministers lead you to grow in single-hearted love?

Describe the worst "minister" you have personally encountered. If you were his spiritual director, how would you help him grow more fully into Christ's single-hearted love?

Which of the dimensions of ministering to the wider world are you yourself living at the present time? Whom would you consider your role model for ministering?

AFTERWORD

Christian chastity is about how body-spirit creatures go about loving God and one another single-heartedly. In its mature form, single-hearted love is loving God, people and the world with God's own love. Experiencing this love brings us face to face with Jesus and how we perceive our relationship with him. Love me, he insists at the Last Supper, and the Father will love you and we will dwell with you. The final integration of this love is thus God himself, the Trinity, the indwelling of the living Trinity of sheer loving in us. We are baptized into this mystery, the mystery of God's single-hearted love. This is the first love, the nucleus of all other loves, the love around which our lives are spiraling, the only love that is true and eternal life.

The way into this life is long and sometimes hard, as Soledad Marinera observes in *Holding Back*:

> Scattered as I am—and tired—
> I can't give all, no holding back,
> day and night over a lifetime.
> I can only give you—in nanoseconds—
> myself,
> in the hope that you'll take me
> and give me away
> in your eager, outflooding gift.

In the end, our desires do matter, the desires that keep opening our hearts to Jesus, so that he can do for us what we cannot—join us to the deepest mystery of our hearts and hold us there by the absolute single-heartedness of his limitless love for the Father and for us. He can and will do in us what we cannot do for ourselves—create an Easter, create a Pentecost and bring us home to our hearts.

APPENDIX 1

POETRY

CINDERELLA

Send your sisters to hell and don't forgive
the furtive whispers, niggling, nibbling calculations.
The standardized measure in Lilliput won't serve–
God's hands are too large and the pot too fine to be made
except by feel, eyes closed, in the song of the wheel.
The open-eyed cant, songless, amiss-taking, mistaking.
Mistake to pause–while wheel sings–to chant regrets.
Don't forgive the delay, send them packing, Cinderella.
The work's in hand.

HERE I AM

Here I am
in free-fall from the lip
of the mother of all waves,
at a loss to remember
what impelled me into the storm,
astounded, beside myself
that in a nanosecond of vision,
as lightning etched your voice
onto the death-dark night–
irresistibly magnetic–
I clambered from a boat already breaking up,
drawn to where you,
striding over the screaming vortices of hell,
all fear groundless,
in a sudden suspended silence–
call me.

LOVE SILENT SWEEPING

Marginal
because I'm moving
from the let's-get-real
rah-rah-rah
to the solitary verge
where love sweeps silent

WHERE

Prophets and virgins
crying the silence in the gateway,
egos ground to optic perfection
revealing you–unmistakably–the Lord of the here
and the there.

APPENDIX 2

MY OWN STORY